# *The* Dogs *of* Camelot

# The Dogs of Camelot

## Stories of the
# KENNEDY CANINES

*Margaret Reed and Joan Lownds*

Foreword by Clint Hill, Assistant Director (Ret.), US Secret Service

Guilford, Connecticut

The Kennedy family on Cape Cod in 1963, with eight of the nine dogs they brought to the White House. CECIL W. STOUGHTON, WHITE HOUSE PHOTOGRAPHS. JOHN F. KENNEDY PRESIDENTIAL LIBRARY AND MUSEUM.

*Dedicated to my Mom, who taught me that nothing was impossible. —Margaret Reed, PhD*

*Dedicated to my dear friend Mary Ann Haran Quinn, "the likes of which we will never see again." —Joan Lownds*

An imprint of The Rowman & Littlefield Publishing Group, Inc.
4501 Forbes Blvd., Ste. 200
Lanham, MD 20706
www.rowman.com

Distributed by NATIONAL BOOK NETWORK

British Library Cataloguing in Publication Information available

**Library of Congress Cataloging-in-Publication Data**

Names: Reed, Margaret A., 1959- author. | Lownds, Joan, author.
Title: The dogs of camelot : stories of the Kennedy canines / Margaret Reed and Joan Lownds ; foreword by Clint Hill, Assistant Director (retired) U.S. Secret Service.
Description: Guilford, Connecticut : Lyons Press, [2018] | Includes bibliographical references and index.
Identifiers: LCCN 2017049365 (print) | LCCN 2018001482 (ebook) | ISBN 9781493031627 (e-book) | ISBN 9781493031610 (hardback) | ISBN 9781493031627 (ebook)
Subjects: LCSH: Kennedy, John F. (John Fitzgerald), 1917-1963. | Dogs—Anecdotes. | Dog owners—Anecdotes. | Human-animal relationships—Anecdotes.
Classification: LCC SF426.2 (ebook) | LCC SF426.2 .R44 2018 (print) | DDC 636.7—dc23
LC record available at https://lccn.loc.gov/2017049365

# CONTENTS

President Kennedy and John Jr. walk beside Caroline as she rides her pony, Macaroni, at Camp David in 1963. ROBERT L. KNUDSEN, WHITE HOUSE PHOTOGRAPHS. JOHN F. KENNEDY PRESIDENTIAL LIBRARY AND MUSEUM.

# FOREWORD

Most homes in the United States have a pet of one type or another, and the White House is no exception. Presidents of the United States beginning with George Washington have had one or more pets, from the common sort—horses, dogs, cats, and canaries—to the more exotic—bobcats, black bears, silkworms, goats, and alligators. No animal seemed to be exempt. During my tenure as a Secret Service agent from 1958 to 1975, I witnessed a vast variety of pets come and go.

I was assigned to Mrs. John F. Kennedy shortly after the election in 1960. The Kennedys lived in the Georgetown section of Washington, DC, and had a pet dog named Charlie and a cat named Tom Kitten. Charlie, a wire-haired Welsh Terrier, was quite protective of his master and mistress until he got to know you. I had to be very careful not to surprise him or he would snarl and appear ready to attack. Tom Kitten was a little sneaky and stayed out of the way most of the time.

On January 20, 1961, President and Mrs. Kennedy moved into the White House. They brought with them Tom Kitten. Their daughter, Caroline, and son, John Jr., remained in Palm

Beach, Florida, because their rooms were not ready. Charlie stayed with Mrs. Kennedy's mother, Mrs. Janet Auchincloss, until the children made the move to the White House in early February. President Kennedy was allergic to cat dander, so it was only a short stay at 1600 Pennsylvania Avenue for Tom Kitten. Mrs. Kennedy arranged for her personal secretary, Mary Gallagher, to host the cat. This made it possible for Caroline to go see him on occasion, and the president did not have to suffer from his allergies.

In June 1961, President and Mrs. Kennedy went to Vienna, Austria, for a meeting with Austrian President Adolf Schärf and talks with Soviet Premier Nikita Khrushchev. The Soviets had had a recent successful space launch that sent some plants and animals into space, including Strelka, a female dog. In a conversation with Premier Khrushchev, Mrs. Kennedy mentioned Strelka, and Khrushchev indicated the dog had recently delivered puppies. Mrs. Kennedy expressed an interest, and a short time later, Pushinka, one of Strelka's pups, arrived at the White House as a gift for the Kennedy family. The puppy was a complete surprise to President Kennedy, who had not been a part of the conversation in Vienna. Charlie, the Welsh Terrier, became very fond of Pushinka, and in the spring of 1963 four mixed-breed pups were added to the Kennedy K-9 corps. Caroline named them Blackie, White Tips, Butterfly, and Streaker.

President and Mrs. Kennedy, Caroline, and Vice President Johnson and his daughter, Lynda Bird Johnson, visit Tex, a pony given to Caroline by the vice president, on the White House grounds in 1962. An unidentified boy sits astride Tex.

This gift of an animal by a foreign leader to the Kennedy White House became contagious, because from that point on, it seemed everyone had something to give. When I was in India with Mrs. Kennedy in 1962, the Indian government presented her with two tiger cubs. She had visions of them roaming the White House grounds, but they ended up in the National Zoo. We traveled on to Pakistan and President Ayub Khan gleefully presented Mrs. Kennedy with a horse named Sardar, which she loved. Sardar was sent to Middleburg, Virginia, and Mrs. Kennedy rode him frequently.

Ireland's president, Eamon de Valera, sent the Kennedys a Connemara pony named Leprechaun and a black-and-white Cocker Spaniel named Shannon, as well as two spotted deer, which ended up in the National Zoo. A priest in Ireland sent an Irish Wolfhound as a gift. Even the president's father, Joseph P. Kennedy, gifted Mrs. Kennedy with a German Shepherd named Clipper.

A common misconception is that Caroline's pony Macaroni was a gift from Vice President Lyndon Johnson. Actually, Caroline already had Macaroni and the pony the vice president gave her was a Yucatan Bay named Tex—a nod to Johnson's home state of Texas.

As the number of canines in the Kennedy kennel increased, it became apparent someone had to be responsible for them. They needed a dog keeper. The chief usher of the White

# THE WHITE HOUSE

For: Mrs. Kennedy

From: Clint Hill


Deputy Chief Albert L. Embrey -- (In charge of all
Canine Corps)

Captain Frank V. Breazeale

Lt. William C. Wright)
                     ) - Share responsibilities.
Lt. John E. Drass   )


March 4, 1963

A note from Secret Service agent Clint Hill about sharing the workload for the
Kennedy K-9 corps in 1963. JACQUELINE BOUVIER KENNEDY ONASSIS PERSONAL
PAPERS. JOHN F. KENNEDY PRESIDENTIAL LIBRARY AND MUSEUM.

House is responsible for the domestic staff and the maintenance personnel working in the White House. J. B. West, the chief usher at the time, selected Traphes Bryant from the electrician staff to add dog keeper to his duties. His job was to see to their grooming, diet, exercise, and overall health.

Some of the happiest times I observed President Kennedy were when he was with his wife, children, and their pets, away from the White House. One or more of the dogs would accompany the family to the Virginia country home in Atoka, or to Palm Beach, or to Hyannis Port.

In the fall of 1963, the president and his family spent a weekend at their new country home near Atoka, near Middleburg, Virginia. On a beautiful afternoon, with the sun shining brightly on the golden leaves falling from the trees, Mrs. Kennedy and Caroline were exhibiting their equestrian skills as the president and guests Ben and Toni Bradlee observed from the residence patio. Mrs. Kennedy rode rapidly across the open fields with Clipper, the German Shepherd, in hot but futile pursuit. Wolfie, the Irish Wolfhound, and Shannon, the Cocker Spaniel, were romping in the patio area. Young John was playing soldier in the woods with his nanny, Maud Shaw, acting as an army nurse.

Upon conclusion of the riding, Mrs. Kennedy brought Leprechaun, Caroline's pony, up on the patio of the house to where the president was seated on the ground. The president

Caroline's pony, Leprechaun, playfully nuzzles President Kennedy at Atoka on November 10, 1963. CECIL W. STOUGHTON, WHITE HOUSE PHOTOGRAPHS. JOHN F. KENNEDY PRESIDENTIAL LIBRARY AND MUSEUM.

apparently had some sort of treat in his hand and the pony smelled it, began to search for it, and started licking and nuzzling him. It was one of the most hilarious scenes I observed while assigned to presidential protection. There were times when the pony's intrusive actions were so intense, I was concerned the president might be injured, but President and Mrs. Kennedy and their guests were bursting with laughter. It is rare for a president to have such a relaxing time. The Kennedy pets gave him and his family the opportunity to really enjoy life to the fullest.

This book, *The Dogs of Camelot: Stories of the Kennedy Canines*, will give you an insight into how much pets help the occupant of the Office of President of the United States. The ability to walk to the Oval Office door, step out onto the colonnade, and watch dogs playing nearby on the White House lawn is a wonderful distraction from the continuous stress a president faces each and every day. Just the ability to reach down and stroke the furry head of a favorite dog can give the president a moment of relief from the daily grind. Dogs have been called man's best friend. When it comes to the presidency, sometimes a dog is the president's only true friend.

—Clint Hill, Assistant Director (Retired)
US Secret Service,
May 23, 2017

# INTRODUCTION

## by Margaret Reed, PhD

Everyone has a story to tell, and this is mine. I happen to love dogs. I also love history, most notably the years when John F. Kennedy was president. One of my very first memories is watching President Kennedy address the nation on our small black-and-white TV, with its crumpled piece of aluminum foil wrapped around the antennae.

President Kennedy was handsome, spoke with an accent that could barely be understood by a kid from New York (which is what I was), and gestured with his hands to emphasize the points he was trying to make. For some reason, I was captivated by him, yet never understood why.

My mother was a dyed-in-the-wool Republican who had campaigned ardently for Richard Nixon. She had a picture of herself with him and displayed it proudly on her desk. "He was the one who should have won," was her constant mantra. (That mantra would shift dramatically after the Watergate hearings.)

Dad had gone to Harvard with Ted Kennedy, and he too shared Mom's belief that the Republican way was the only way. He never spoke well of Ted Kennedy, yet for some reason, I was never influenced by his nay-saying. In fact, it made me more determined to find out who the Kennedys were and why my parents were so adamantly opposed to them.

In the summer of 1963, Mom rented a house on Cape Cod. The house was in Hyannis Port, a small village by Lewis Bay, with sweeping views of the sparkling blue Atlantic Ocean. To this day, when I return to that beach, I feel transported back in time to a feeling of serenity from those summers.

Those of us who are fond of history tend to want to relive the past, seeing where we have been, where we are now, and how those decisions shaped our future. I can tell you from my own past that those days set the course for the life I now live. I believe that no meetings are simply chance—that everyone and everything that happens in our lives is preordained by destiny. Little did I know that my destiny would be forged on an August day in 1963.

—

He was enormous. The black-and-tan police dog that ventured into the yard of our rental home was the largest dog I had ever seen. As I sat on the ground pulling weeds, he meandered over to me with a slobber-covered ball. He kept pushing the ball in my direction, pleading with eyes that said, "Throw the ball! Throw the ball!" But as I slowly reached for the ball, he would quickly grab it and start the process all over again.

Close-up of Clipper on the White House grounds with Mrs. Kennedy in 1963.
CECIL W. STOUGHTON, WHITE HOUSE PHOTOGRAPHS. JOHN F. KENNEDY PRESIDENTIAL
LIBRARY AND MUSEUM.

My mother raced into the yard and yelled to the dog, "Go home! Go home!" The dog didn't pay any attention to her but instead lay down right in front of me. My mother's protective instinct kicked in, and she told me not to move.

Almost instantaneously, two men in dark suits came up the walkway, beckoning, "Clipper, here boy, here boy." The massive dog quickly got up, took his ball, and off they went. The men apologized profusely for his behavior—and for taking ten years off my mother's life. Being the Irishwoman she was, she let them know in no uncertain terms that she would call the police if this kind of incident ever happened again, and that they should be more responsible with their dog. What we didn't know at the time was who the dog's owner was, or who these men were.

I only knew that I was sad to see the dog leave and confused as to why Mom had become so angry and upset. At no time did I ever feel threatened by this dog. He just seemed to be like any dog that wanted to play ball. Not having a dog of my own, I was desperately happy whenever the opportunity of canine companionship presented itself. However, I endured the familiar lecture of how strange dogs should be avoided at all costs due to the various diseases they might carry or, worse yet, a bite they might deliver. Those words fell upon deaf ears as I waited eagerly for the next encounter with the next "strange" dog. As much as I begged for a dog, at that point in my life it just wasn't going to happen.

**Clipper stands on the White House West Wing lawn in 1963.** CECIL W. STOUGHTON, WHITE HOUSE PHOTOGRAPHS. JOHN F. KENNEDY PRESIDENTIAL LIBRARY AND MUSEUM.

They say that truth is stranger than fiction. In my experience, those words never held more meaning than what followed the encounter with the police dog named Clipper. Our next-door neighbor informed Mom that the dog was perfectly safe and, in fact, belonged to the president of the United States. She said it wasn't uncommon to see the Kennedy dogs wandering the neighborhood and that it was usually the Secret Service men who had to retrieve the errant canines. Still, Mom was convinced that children and strange dogs didn't mix, and it wasn't proper for them to be running loose in the neighborhood. (I've often wondered since if she would have felt differently if it was the Nixons' dog, Checkers.)

The following day, a man arrived at the house to once again apologize for frightening our family and inquire as to whether I would like to see some puppies. I was terribly excited, but Mom said no at first. I begged and pleaded with her and finally wore her down. I have no doubt it was the tears that finally persuaded her.

My mother and I walked across the street with this man, whose name was Bob, to the Kennedy Compound. Bob genuinely seemed to like children and was very concerned about my earlier incident with Clipper. He assured us that the dog was harmless but simply obsessed with balls and sticks. I told him I wasn't scared but my mom had been. Perhaps sensing my deep affection for canines, he then told me that there were

**Pushinka and her puppies on the White House lawn in 1963.** CECIL W. STOUGHTON,
WHITE HOUSE PHOTOGRAPHS. JOHN F. KENNEDY PRESIDENTIAL LIBRARY AND MUSEUM.

lots of dogs in the neighborhood that ran free. This was the
most exciting news of the day! It meant there were plenty of
dogs for me to play with.

The compound's expansive green lawn presented the perfect place for dogs and puppies of all sizes to play. From large to small, everywhere you looked, there were dogs, including the four pups we had been invited to see. Two had already been spoken for, but the other two still needed homes. Of course, I asked if we could have one, but the expected reply of "No, you can't have a dog" sprang from my mother's lips once again.

Then the tall, handsome man I'd seen on TV appeared. He greeted us and asked how we liked the puppies. His eyes were greenish gray, and his chestnut red hair was slightly windblown. There are some people you like instantly, and he was certainly one of them. He introduced us to the group of children who were with him, and then politely thanked us for stopping by. Even Mom was impressed.

The significance of such moments is lost on children. At that age, I just wanted to play with the dogs. Where was Clipper? I was told he was at the other house. I really liked him best and wanted to throw his slime-covered ball for him. When it was time to go, I looked back at the handsome man as he drove a golf cart full of children up the driveway, followed by the raucous enthusiasm of a pack of dogs. Then they were gone. In that brief moment, I knew I had experienced something extraordinary. I've never forgotten that day.

# Chapter One

# For the
# Love of Dogs

Looking at the picture of the little boy in the white sun hat with a Newfoundland by his side, it's hard to imagine that he would one day become the thirty-fifth president of the United States. The photograph shows clearly that little Jack Kennedy shared a close bond with this canine companion

For Rose and Joe Kennedy Sr. and their nine children, dogs were cherished fixtures of family life. One of these canine companions from President Kennedy's childhood was the irrepressible Buddy. He lived with the Kennedys until they moved from Brookline to Riverdale, New York, and Buddy was re-homed to a family who lived on a farm near Cape Cod, where he would have space to roam.

One of the members of Buddy's new family was Priscilla Harris, and she wrote a letter to Senator Ted Kennedy on

John F. Kennedy with his dog Buddy at Hyannis Port, Massachusetts in 1925.
JOHN F. KENNEDY LIBRARY FOUNDATION

December 12, 1969, on file at the John F. Kennedy Library Foundation, that paints a vivid picture of the energetic Newfoundland dog and the Kennedy family's strong connection with him.

Priscilla lived on a farm and cranberry bog in the small village of Duxbury, which sits on the South Shore, along the eastern border of Cape Cod Bay. Since Priscilla's home was along the main route to the Cape in those days, many wealthy summer folk stopped by to purchase fresh eggs and produce. To Priscilla and her family, most of these summer people were virtually indistinguishable—and their children complied with the old adage to be seen and not heard, sitting properly and upright in the front seat while they waited in the car with their nursemaid.

However, the Kennedy family was strikingly different, with the hands-on parenting style of Joe Sr. and Rose and the high spirits of the children. When Priscilla first saw the Kennedys, several children spilled out of a Rolls-Royce and ran exuberantly around the farm with their mother—not a nursemaid. The children's father, Joe Sr., "came to the kitchen door and asked my mother [Matilda Swanson] if we had any fresh eggs, vegetables, and fruits," Priscilla recalled. "He bought a tremendous amount of everything we had, and tipped his hat to my mother when he left. The children had been running around, having fun, while being carefully watched by their mother."

The Harris family grew more acquainted with the Kennedys during the course of their regular summer visits, with Joe Sr. often sitting in their kitchen and having coffee with them. Then one day Priscilla's father, the Reverend Emil Olaf Swanson, received a letter from Joe Kennedy Sr. asking if they wanted to adopt Buddy. The Kennedys were planning to move from Brookline to New York, and they didn't want Buddy in a kennel because he was used to running free. Also, Buddy was belligerent around other dogs.

The Harris family didn't have a dog at the time, and they urged their father to agree to adopt Buddy. Reverend Swanson acquiesced, and the family drove to Brookline to pick up Buddy—where they were astonished by what they saw. Priscilla described him as "a huge black creature, the likes of which we had never seen, except in pictures. He greeted us all like old friends and straightaway became one of the family."

However, Buddy's combativeness around other dogs became a problem. He would often attack two or three dogs at once, and usually one of them would go for his throat. Priscilla recalled a time when Buddy and two collies held up traffic for miles while engaged in a ferocious fight in the middle of the road. The melee was so dramatic that people got out of their cars and watched, and a state policeman pulled out his revolver and would have shot Buddy had it not been for Priscilla's pleadings.

Buddy had arrived with a wide collar with copper studs and a large metal plate that read "Joe and Jack Kennedy, 131 Naples Road, Brookline, Mass. Lic 1276." More than once that heavy collar saved his life.

The Kennedys often came to visit Buddy, but there was one time that stood out in sharp relief when Joe Sr. brought his two oldest sons, who were teenagers at the time. Because Buddy was such a fighter, the police had ordered the Harrises to tie him up. The undaunted canine broke the rope he was tied with more than once, and on that particular day he was attached to his doghouse with a chain.

To Priscilla, it was obvious from their expressions that the three Kennedys didn't approve of Buddy being tethered like this, and she attempted to explain why he needed to be.

When Buddy saw the boys, he greeted them excitedly by standing on his hind legs and throwing his front paws on their shoulders, almost as if he was embracing them. "There was no doubt he remembered them," Priscilla wrote in her letter. However, a chagrined Mr. Kennedy told the boys not to let Buddy put his muddy paws on their clean shirts.

When it was time to leave, Joe Jr. and Jack appeared sad to Priscilla. She had the impression that they wanted to rescue Buddy and take him back to Hyannis Port. Because both boys were handsome, Priscilla felt self-conscious and didn't tell them that Buddy wasn't always chained, and that she and her family took him for long walks through the woods, which he really enjoyed. But after they left, she wished she had.

After several years, the Kennedy family stopped coming to the farm. Priscilla read a newspaper account about their move to London, where Joe Sr. served as the US Ambassador to England from 1938 to 1940.

Meanwhile, Buddy lived a long life with the Harris family, until one cold winter night when they let him out and he did not come back. Priscilla's brother went looking for him but didn't find him until the next morning. Because Buddy didn't have a scratch on him, they concluded that he had died of a heart attack. By this time the Harrises had lost touch with the Kennedys, except for the stories they read about them in the newspapers. The news about them had turned tragic, with the death in 1944 of Joe Jr., a bomber pilot who was killed in action in World War II, followed by the death of his sister Kathleen, also in a plane crash, in 1948.

To Priscilla and her family, the reports were heartbreaking, perhaps because of their special bond with the Kennedys through Buddy. "My mother wept over their tragedies—the ones she knew about," Priscilla wrote. "She would say 'Oh no, not that beautiful child.' My mother died before the two assassinations, and we were glad she didn't know about them. It might have shaken her great faith in mankind, for where the Kennedys were concerned, as in most other things, she had very strong feelings."

—

In the summer of 1937, Jack Kennedy and his best friend from boarding school, Lemoyne "Lem" Billings, set off for a three-month tour of Europe, where the atmosphere was volatile due to Adolf Hitler's ascendant Nazi regime. Joe Kennedy Sr. had urged them to take the trip as an educational experience before tensions boiled over into war. Both young men were twenty years old and Ivy Leaguers—Jack was at Harvard and Lem was at Princeton. They brought with them a Ford Cabriolet, and as they drove throughout France to Italy and Germany, both young men kept journals of their observations.

The mood in Germany was rife with anti-American sentiment. In the book *Jack and Lem* by David Pitts, Jack described an unpleasant episode in this way: "August 20– Friday–Nuremberg, Wurtenberg. Started out as usual, only this time we had the added attraction of being spit on."

Still, Jack tried to understand as much as possible about the country, and one aspect of his plan was to pick up every German hitchhiker he saw. "This worked out very well because a high percentage of them were students and could speak English," Lem noted. "In that way, we [Jack] learned a great deal about Germany. I remember picking up two German soldiers who were on leave. . . . They were with us for a week and we gathered that their general attitude was pro-Hitler. We picked up another German student who was very anti-Hitler. He is probably dead now."

Except for their efforts with the hitchhikers, Jack and Lem found that most of their cordial overtures toward the German people fell flat. Lem recalled that the most of the Germans they met were "insufferable . . . We just had awful experiences there. They were just so haughty and sure of themselves."

The only friend they made came in the form of a self-assured Dachshund puppy they purchased on their way to Nuremberg. Jack's diary entry on this was: "August 19— Stopped on the way and bought a Dachshund of great beauty for $8.00 as a present for Olive [his girlfriend at this time]. Immediately got hay fever, etc., so it looks like the odds are 8-1 towards 'Offie' getting to America." "Offie" was the name of the secretary to the American ambassador in Paris, and the young men believed the puppy bore a resemblance to her.

The dog was also known as "Dunker", the only German word Jack and Lem knew, which literally means "a member of the German church of the Brethren." They referred to their new traveling companion as "the nicest German they had ever met."

But Jack's allergic reaction to the dog worsened as the trip went on. According to the book *Jack and Lem* by David Pitts, Lem wrote, "The dachshund gave him asthma. It was a new malady to add to his already long medical history."

The future president with Dunker, the Dachshund puppy he acquired during a summer trip to Germany in 1937 with his friend Lem Billings. Jack and Lem described Dunker as the only friend they made on the trip. COLLECTION. JOHN F. KENNEDY PRESIDENTIAL LIBRARY AND MUSEUM.

Still, the future president could not bear to part ways with the handsome Dachshund, who strutted and swaggered when he was among other canines. Even the unfriendly Germans had a soft spot for Offie, as Lem observed: "They weren't very appreciative of Americans, having heard all the propaganda about the United States on the radio, but for Offie they had a soft spot." Ultimately, Jack had no choice but to leave Offie behind, not only because of his allergies, but also because Offie would not be allowed to cross the border. Lem wrote that a "heartsick" Jack "delayed the parting as long as he could," but the results of an allergy test came back positive, indicating that Offie was the cause. (Jack would later be treated by allergists, which allowed him to maintain his relationships with his beloved canines.)

—

Wherever the future president traveled, a dog was never far behind. During one of his visits to the Jay-6 Cattle Ranch in Benson, Arizona, his canine companion was a Doberman Pinscher named Moe. Jack had gone to Arizona for the sake of his fragile health, after Joe Kennedy Sr. decided that the hearty ranch life under the Arizona sun would benefit him. So Joe Sr. sent Jack on a working vacation. He rode fence and herded cattle, according to historian Jim Turner. This "ranch cure" proved effective because when Jack went to Harvard in the fall, he joined his brother Joe on the Harvard football team.

When Jack left Arizona, he arranged for Moe to be shipped to his family in Hyannis Port. Ted Kennedy described a memorable meeting in 1946 with the boisterous Doberman in his book, *True Compass*: "A delivery truck brought the dog to our house from the railroad station. A note fixed to the crate read, 'My name is Moe and I don't bite.' When I looked at Moe through the slats, I was glad for that news, because Moe was one big, muscular dog."

However, as the fourteen-year-old Ted opened the crate, Moe bounded out, nipped him, and raced across the lawn. "He circled a bit and then made for the McKelvey house next door. Johnny McKelvey, a boy a little younger than me, was standing in his yard, eyes riveted on Moe. Moe bore in on Johnny and sent him flying like a tenpin in a bowling alley. Johnny started to bawl. His nanny came rushing out of the house and screamed, 'Get up Johnny! Get up! Your mother doesn't want you to ruin those nice new pants! You're getting a grass stain on them!' Johnny couldn't stop howling. Moe, meanwhile, was having a hell of a good time. He came charging back up to our house, tongue and tail waving," Ted Kennedy wrote. "The delivery truck man, a true profile in courage, crouched, spread his arms, and somehow managed to grab him."

Joe Kennedy Sr. had been monitoring the scene, and told Ted in no uncertain terms to "put him back in that crate and

John F. Kennedy, left, is shown with his brother Robert and his dog, Moe, in Hyannis Port, Massachusetts, in 1946. ASSOCIATED PRESS PHOTO

ship him back!" The youngest Kennedy was happy to oblige. "It gave me a rare chance to tease Jack," Ted recounted.

The headstrong Doberman also left a lasting impression on Jack's cousin, Tom Fitzgerald Jr. In his book, *Grandpa Stories*, written for members of the Fitzgerald and Kennedy families, Tom described a striking memory of Moe from the days when Jack had a room at the Bellevue Hotel in Boston, where their grandfather, John Francis ("Honey Fitz") Fitzgerald, had taken up residence. (Honey Fitz was the father of Jack's mother, Rose, and he had been the mayor of Boston and a US congressman.)

Moe and Jack were constant companions—until he went missing one day. The popular and well-known Honey Fitz assured Jack that he would find him, according to Tom. So the three of them headed to Boston Common, where Honey Fitz asked everyone he encountered if they had seen Moe.

Eventually Moe did turn up. "He was found because people knew who Grandpa was, and what they needed to do for him," Tom explained. "He carried that aura about him."

—

Following the marriage of then-senator Jack Kennedy to Jacqueline Bouvier in 1953, the newlyweds lived in the upscale Georgetown section of Washington, DC. Eventually the couple moved to Hickory Hill in McLean, Virginia, an elegant eighteen-room white brick Georgian mansion, surrounded by acres of rolling lawns dotted with massive oak and hickory trees. The home seemed to be the perfect setting for the large family they envisioned having. Not surprisingly, given the young senator's history, they soon acquired a dog—an exuberant Golden Retriever they named Tippy. Long before this breed became one of America's most popular dogs, the Kennedys were once again trendsetters.

According to the oral history of Mrs. Janet Auchincloss, the mother of Mrs. Kennedy, provided for the JFK Library, Jack loved to play with Tippy outdoors, but suffered with his allergies if the dog ventured inside Hickory Hill. However, she noted that Jack bore the allergies stoically.

The two years that the couple spent at Hickory Hill were tumultuous. On August 17, 1956, Jack's bid for the Democratic vice presidential nomination failed. Six days later, the couple's daughter, Arabella, was stillborn at a Newport, Rhode Island, hospital.

By the following year, they had sold Hickory Hill to Jack's brother, Bobby, who had a rapidly growing family, and moved back to Georgetown. Tippy remained with Jack and Jacqueline at first, and his boisterous energy provided comic relief during the couple's 1957 appearance on a talk show called *Home*, hosted by TV personality Arlene Francis.

The show begins with Francis and Mrs. Kennedy sitting in the Kennedy town house, with the soft-spoken future First

John, Robert, and Ethel Kennedy with Tippy at Hickory Hill.
THE LIFE PICTURE COLLECTION/GETTY IMAGES. PHOTOGRAPHER: PAUL SCHUTZER.

Lady dressed in a black dress and pearls. Francis asks her about her life as a senator's wife, focusing mainly on her domestic duties. Mrs. Kennedy seems to chafe under the questions that frame her as a housewife, which was not what she had described as her goal when she was a senior at Miss Porter's School. Arlene even asks Mrs. Kennedy—who spoke several languages and had degrees in French literature and American history—if she is "interested in politics." Mrs. Kennedy seems taken aback, and says that she is.

Francis then follows her on a round of domestic errands: taking Jack's shoes to the cobbler and his suits to the cleaners, and buying meat at a butcher shop, although she professes to not be a great cook. Tippy accompanies Mrs. Kennedy on these errands, tugging on the leash and bounding ahead, providing a classic image of a dog walking its owner and causing Francis to remark, "That dog is more powerful than you are!"

When they walk to a park, Mrs. Kennedy lets Tippy off his leash, and he bolts toward a group of small children playing in a sandbox, promptly knocking one of them over. Back at the town house, Mrs. Kennedy opens the back door and Tippy bursts into the tiny garden, bounding around in circles. "He's used to the country," Mrs. Kennedy explains.

Next, Senator Kennedy, dressed in a dark suit, white shirt, and tie, joins his wife on their sofa as they sip coffee and answer more questions. The poised young senator offers a glimpse into the eloquent president he will become, saying it is a "serious time for the US but . . . if people exercise good citizenship the country can look ahead with a good deal of confidence and hope." Tippy then charges into the room and climbs onto Jack's lap, which makes him grin happily for the only time during the strained and awkward interview.

Soon after, Tippy would go to live with Jack's mother-in-law and her family on their Merrywood estate in McLean, Virginia, where he had more room to roam and play. Eventually, Tippy joined Tom Kitten and the Gallagher family in Alexandria, Virginia. Mrs. Auchincloss recalled how Jack would frequently visit "to just call on Tippy. He would come out and not even tell us he was there. He just wanted to pet his dog and talk to him. He really loved animals desperately."

**Schoolchildren visiting the White House pose with Charlie in 1962.**
ROBERT L. KNUDSEN, WHITE HOUSE PHOTOGRAPHS. JOHN F. KENNEDY PRESIDENTIAL
LIBRARY AND MUSEUM.

# Chapter Two

# President Kennedy's Most Beloved Dog

In the private residence at the Kennedy White House, family life bustled with a collection of pets that included as many as nine dogs at one time, a cat, parakeets, hamsters, rabbits, deer, and seven horses. This unparalleled multitude of animals at 1600 Pennsylvania Avenue came as no surprise to those who knew the president and Mrs. Jacqueline Kennedy. Ever since they were children, their love of animals had been one of the singular themes of their lives. The American public only saw glimpses of the many Kennedy pets, however, most likely because of the way Mrs. Kennedy zealously guarded her family's privacy.

The beloved pets of Camelot played key roles in the Kennedy presidency. For example, in his book, *Dog Days at the White House*, the White House kennel keeper, Traphes Bryant, described a remarkable event that took place at the height of the Cuban missile crisis: "I was there in Jack Kennedy's office that day. Everything was in an uproar. . . . There was talk about the Russian fleet coming in and our fleet blocking them off. It looked like war. Out of the blue, Kennedy suddenly called for Charlie to be brought to his office."

According to Bryant, "After petting his Welsh Terrier for a while, President Kennedy relaxed, returned Charlie to the kennel keeper, and calmly said, 'I suppose that it's time to make some decisions.'"

Charlie was the president's most beloved dog. He adorned magazine covers and appeared in countless news stories. He was born on November 30, 1959, at the Port Fortune Kennels in Osterville, Massachusetts, with a pedigree that was stellar among his breed and had descended from the famous Strathglass line of Welsh Terriers—among the best America had to offer. His registered name was Port Fortune's Sarah's Ben, but to all who knew him, he was simply Charlie.

Charlie began his life with the Kennedy family when he was purchased by Ambassador Joseph P. Kennedy's niece, Ann Gargan, on May 10, 1960. Ann was a lover of all animals, especially dogs, and would play a key part in assembling the

John Jr. and other children with Charlie at the White House Easter egg roll in 1963.
CECIL W. STOUGHTON, WHITE HOUSE PHOTOGRAPHS. JOHN F. KENNEDY PRESIDENTIAL
LIBRARY AND MUSEUM.

future Kennedy K-9 corps. Charlie was then given to Caroline
Kennedy as a gift in the summer of 1960. Her grandfather
believed that terriers, especially Welsh ones, were great companions for children. Charlie was the first of many dogs that
would call the Kennedy White House home.

President Kennedy with Charlie, John Jr., and Paul "Red" Fay, Undersecretary of the Navy, at Camp David in 1963. ROBERT L. KNUDSEN, WHITE HOUSE PHOTOGRAPHS. JOHN F. KENNEDY PRESIDENTIAL LIBRARY AND MUSEUM.

As a breed, Welsh Terriers have often been described as mischievous and full of energy. The American Kennel Club breed standard to this day describes the Welsh Terrier's personality as "friendly, outgoing to people and other dogs, showing spirit and courage." This description could also have been used to describe Charlie's new family.

As the First Family's dog, Charlie became famous in his own right. An adoring American public was ravenous for all things Kennedy, including the animals that shared their lives. Rarely had such an amalgam of youth, wit, and glamour characterized a presidency, and the media coverage was equally unprecedented.

When Charlie arrived at the Kennedy Compound in Hyannis Port, he quickly made his presence known. He was a lively, feisty pup who would challenge anyone and anything that hindered him from what he wanted at any particular moment. Caroline and Charlie got along famously and often appeared together in various media outlets, causing Charlie to become a standard-bearer of his breed.

In 1963, in a Welsh Terrier breed column in the *AKC Gazette*, Jack Baird wrote that "Caroline likes Charlie best of all the First Family dogs. As Mrs. Kennedy used to show dogs when she was a young lady, especially with the Bouviers, she should know how important dogs are to children of all ages." Charlie was so popular that during

John Jr. plays with Charlie on the White House lawn in 1963.
ROBERT L. KNUDSEN, WHITE HOUSE PHOTOGRAPHS. JOHN F. KENNEDY PRESIDENTIAL
LIBRARY AND MUSEUM.

the Kennedy years, there was a spike in registrations for the Welsh Terrier breed.

Charlie traveled more than any canine of his generation. Flying on candidate Kennedy's private plane, the *Caroline*, he was a frequent passenger from Hyannis Port to Washington, DC, to Palm Beach. He was regarded as a cherished family member, and in some cases, he was treated better than the men in the president's administration.

On Valentine's Day in 1961, White House social secretary Letitia Baldrige asked Mrs. Kennedy to which men in the president's administration would she would like to send a Valentine's card. She responded that the only man she wanted to send a card was Charlie. Baldrige was dumbfounded by the response and sent no Valentine's Day cards that year.

There was never a dull moment in the life of the president's dog. One of Charlie's favorite pastimes was to herd the ducks and goldfish that swam in the water fountain just outside the White House. He would watch them closely and then suddenly spring into action to see which one he could capture. Eventually, when the activity developed into obsessive-compulsive behavior, a fence was erected around the fountain to protect the seasonal residents, leaving Charlie to terrorize his next unsuspecting victims—who turned out to be the gardeners and maintenance workers.

Mrs. Kennedy, Caroline, and a marine board Air Force Two with Charlie in 1962.

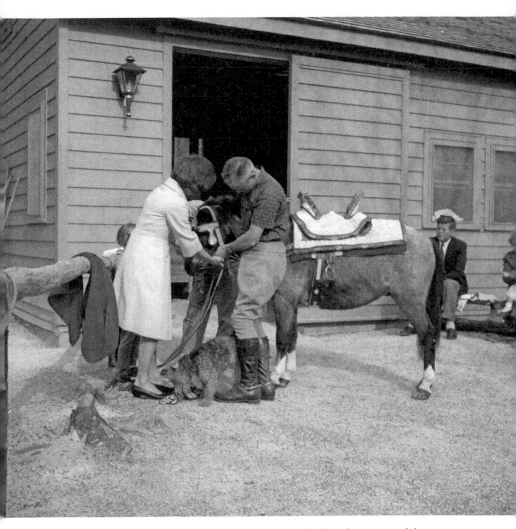

Mrs. Kennedy with Clay T. "Barney" Brittle, and Charlie and Macaroni, while President Kennedy looks on, at Atoka in 1963. ROBERT L. KNUDSEN, WHITE HOUSE PHOTOGRAPHS. JOHN F. KENNEDY PRESIDENTIAL LIBRARY AND MUSEUM.

Charlie eyes the pardoned White House turkey in 1962. The turkey had been saved from becoming someone's Thanksgiving dinner. COLLECTION. JOHN F. KENNEDY PRESIDENTIAL LIBRARY AND MUSEUM.

Facing page: John Jr. on the stairs of the children's tree house in the backyard of the White House in 1963. Standing on the right is his nanny, Maud Shaw, beside White House maître d'hôtel Charles E. Ficklin, along with Charlie. HAROLD SELLERS, WHITE HOUSE PHOTOGRAPHS. JOHN F. KENNEDY PRESIDENTIAL LIBRARY AND MUSEUM.

Charlie also brought his aquatic skills to the White House pool. President Kennedy's doctor prescribed swimming to help his ailing back, and Charlie accompanied him on his daily visits to the pool, swimming alongside him

It seems that almost every detail of Charlie's life with the Kennedys turned into front-page news, including a cover story in the July 1962 *Woman's Day* magazine. The story, by Hilda Cole Espy, describes Charlie's living arrangements at the White House: "Charlie, who came into Caroline's life when she was a year old, lives in a doghouse under a magnolia tree behind the White House (he was never housetrained!). The decision for him to live out of doors came because Charlie, who had been raised in the Kennedys' Georgetown home and at Cape Cod, was accustomed to running in and out of the house to the yard. But the family quarters are on an upper story of the White House and are reached by an elevator."

After playing with Charlie and the other White House pets all day, Caroline used to love watching the TV show *Lassie* with her playmate, Sally Fay, daughter of Kennedy family friend and undersecretary of the Navy, Paul "Red" Fay. "When we were at Camp David, we would watch *Lassie*, and when Lassie lifted her paw at the end of the show, as if to shake hands or wave goodbye, we would mimic Lassie," recalled Fay.

John Jr., Mrs. Kennedy, and Toni Bradlee sit with Charlie at the White House fountain in 1963. Charlie loved to chase the ducks that swam here.

Charlie in front of the White House in 1962.
ROBERT L. KNUDSEN, WHITE HOUSE PHOTOGRAPHS.
JOHN F. KENNEDY PRESIDENTIAL LIBRARY AND MUSEUM.

In spite of his attachment to Charlie and the other family dogs, President Kennedy was actually allergic to dogs—which few people knew. Since the sight of a doctor's frequent visits to the White House might raise the nation's concern, Dr. Paul de Gara, the allergist, used to stride into the presidential residence carrying the necessary medication in an ordinary attaché case—resembling a typical politician in Washington, DC.

After the president's assassination, Mrs. Kennedy and the children lived in the Georgetown home of Averell Harriman, a diplomat and former governor of New York. They then moved to Manhattan, so it was not easy to keep all the dogs, and Mrs. Kennedy found it necessary to place all but Shannon, the Cocker Spaniel, in other homes. She decided that Secret Service agent Bob Foster should have Charlie for his own children to enjoy. Mrs. Kennedy made carefully reasoned decisions as to who would receive the family dogs. She wanted to make sure that their new families would provide them with the love and attention they had received during their time with her family.

In describing Charlie, Mrs. Foster said, "Charlie was his own personality—high energy and very opinionated about life." She further referred to Charlie as "the epitome of an alpha male. He was an obsessive-compulsive dog when it came to balls and sticks." According to Mrs. Foster, "You could throw the ball for him all day and he would never get tired or stop. He was a really independent character with a nice disposition towards children."

Bob Foster stayed on with Mrs. Kennedy and the children for a year following the president's death, but was then reassigned in 1965 due to concerns that the Kennedy children had become too attached to their Secret Service agents. When the Foster family moved back to Ohio, Charlie went with them but had difficulty adjusting to his new home. He was used to the freedom that the White House afforded him with no fenced yard, so he was constantly running away and looking for female dogs in season. The local police frequently picked him up, and he gained a reputation around town as a "ladies' man."

There were strict leash laws in 1965 when Charlie took off for his last and final conquest, again disappearing for a few days. When the police called to say Charlie had found another mate, it was time for the Fosters to make some hard decisions about his future. Despite his wandering, he protected the children fiercely and would not even allow the mailman access to the family's mailbox. In fact, when the mailman saw Charlie outside, he would not deliver the mail.

To further complicate the situation, Charlie never became house-trained and it had become a worsening problem. The difficult decision was finally made to find Charlie a new home. The children and Bob described themselves as heart-broken over this turn of events.

Charlie then went to live with the Trautweins, an older couple who owned a farm in Ohio. Here, the exuberant Welsh Terrier who had brought so much joy to the Kennedys had plenty of room to roam and chase balls and sticks—and perhaps a few ducks.

## Chapter Three

# The Dog Who Liked to "Eat" Reporters

While President Kennedy forged a bond with Charlie, it was Clipper who claimed a special part of Mrs. Kennedy's heart. She loved to walk him around the White House grounds, and United Press International correspondent Merriman Smith described a memorable encounter on an icy winter day in January 1963, according to the *Washington Post* on January 27, 1963.

As Smith was walking across the hard turf of the White House grounds, his head down against the sharp gusts of wind, he suddenly noticed "a casually dressed young woman,

Facing page: The children and Clipper near the White House Christmas tree in 1962.
CECIL W. STOUGHTON, WHITE HOUSE PHOTOGRAPHS. JOHN F. KENNEDY PRESIDENTIAL LIBRARY AND MUSEUM.

hair blowing in the wind, bundled in a well-cut camel's hair polo coat over trim slacks and wearing dark sunglasses. The day was anything but bright." Tugging at the leash wrapped around her wrist was a spirited young black-and-tan German Shepherd. When Smith "snapped his fingers to get the attention of the woman's young police dog, suddenly another man came seemingly out of nowhere, positioning himself quickly between the two strollers until the woman was well beyond him." The woman was Mrs. Jacqueline Kennedy out for one of her walks with Clipper, her beloved dog, and the man was her Secret Service agent.

Those who knew him reported that you could often hear Clipper long before you saw him. His bark was like a running commentary on everything that presented itself to him. He roamed the White House grounds and the Kennedy Compound in Hyannis Port as if he owned them, digging holes in the lawn, grabbing children's toys, and chasing any ball he could find.

Along with his playfulness, Clipper was also characterized by the qualities of his breed. German Shepherds are known for their loyalty, courage, and ability to cross-train for a number of specialized services. They are often used as patrol and detection dogs by police officers and the military, as guide dogs for the blind, as protection dogs, and as search-and-rescue dogs. They also serve the important role of devoted companion and family protector.

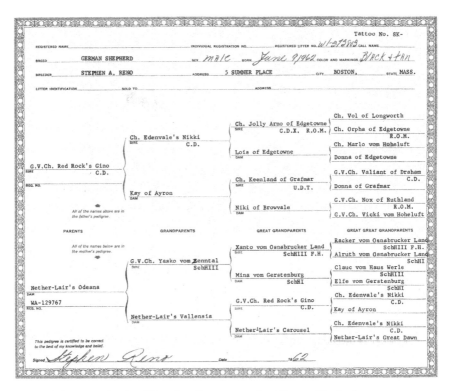

Tattoo No. SK-

REGISTERED NAME _____ INDIVIDUAL REGISTRATION NO. _____ REGISTERED LITTER NO. _WI-373863_ CALL NAME _____

BREED ____ GERMAN SHEPHERD ____ SEX _MALE_ BORN _June 9/1962_ COLOR AND MARKINGS _Black + Tan_

BREEDER ____ STEPHEN A. RENO ____ ADDRESS __5 SUMNER PLACE__ CITY _BOSTON,_ STATE _MASS._

LITTER IDENTIFICATION _____ SOLD TO _____ ADDRESS _____

|  | PARENTS | GRANDPARENTS | GREAT GRANDPARENTS | GREAT GREAT GRANDPARENTS |
|---|---|---|---|---|
|  |  |  |  | Ch. Vol of Longworth |
|  |  |  | Ch. Jolly Arno of Edgetowne C.D.X. R.O.M. | Ch. Orpha of Edgetowne R.O.M. |
|  |  | Ch. Edenvale's Nikki C.D. |  | Ch. Marlo vom Hoheluft |
|  |  |  | Lois of Edgetowne | Donna of Edgetowne |
|  | G.V.Ch. Red Rock's Gino C.D. REG. NO. |  |  | G.V.Ch. Valiant of Draham C.D. |
|  |  |  | Ch. Keenland of Grafmar U.D.T. | Donna of Grafmar |
|  | All of the names above are in the father's pedigree. | Kay of Ayron |  | G.V.Ch. Nox of Ruthland R.O.M. |
|  |  |  | Niki of Browvale | G.V.Ch. Vicki vom Hoheluft |

|  |  |  | GREAT GREAT GRANDPARENTS |
|---|---|---|---|
| All of the names below are in the mother's pedigree. |  |  | Racker vom Osnabrucker Land SchHIII F.H. |
|  | G.V.Ch. Yasko vom Zenntal SchHIII | Xanto vom Osnabrucker Land SchHIII F.H. | Alruth vom Osnabrucker Land SchHI |
|  |  |  | Clauc vom Haus Werle SchHIII |
|  |  | Mina vom Gerstenburg SchHI | Elfe vom Gerstenburg SchHI |
| Nether-Lair's Odeana DAM WA-129767 |  | G.V.Ch. Red Rock's Gino C.D. | Ch. Edenvale's Nikki C.D. |
|  | Nether-Lair's Vallensia |  | Kay of Ayron |
|  |  |  | Ch. Edenvale's Nikki C.D. |
|  |  | Nether-Lair's Carousel | Nether-Lair's Great Dawn |

This pedigree is certified to be correct
to the best of my knowledge and belief.

Signed _Stephen Reno_ Date _____ 19_62_

A document showing Clipper's pedigree as a purebred German Shepherd.

Clipper's official registration certificate in 1962. JACQUELINE BOUVIER KENNEDY
ONASSIS PERSONAL PAPERS. JOHN F. KENNEDY PRESIDENTIAL LIBRARY AND MUSEUM.

Clipper was born on June 9, 1962, and originally purchased by Ann Gargan from Stephan Reno of Roxbury,
Massachusetts, at the Nether-Lair Kennel. It was long
believed that Clipper was bred at the Grafmar German
Shepherd Kennels, whose reputation was recognized interna-
tionally. Although he did not originate at Grafmar, Clipper
was descended from some of their top dogs, as seen in his
three-generation pedigree. He arrived in Hyannis Port on
October 13, 1962, to begin a short but storied life.

This strapping, rambunctious puppy began life as a
Kennedy by virtually destroying the home at their compound
in Hyannis Port. The president's father, Ambassador Joseph
Kennedy, who was wheelchair-bound after suffering a stroke
in 1961, was constantly being bruised by the obstreperous

pup, so finally Ann Gargan and Rose Kennedy decided that Clipper should become Jacqueline Kennedy's companion. Ambassador Kennedy also believed that Clipper would provide the special protection that only a German Shepherd dog could offer.

After the Thanksgiving holiday in 1962, the First Family returned to Washington on Air Force One with Clipper in tow. Meanwhile, First Dog Charlie was relegated to ride in the US Air Force C-130 cargo plane. No doubt Charlie was none too pleased about this turn of events.

While on the plane back to Washington, the venerable White House reporter Helen Thomas sent a query to Mrs. Kennedy, asking her what Clipper liked to eat. Her one-word response was, "Reporters."

Clipper delighted in his new home, especially as Christmas drew near. The White House tree was beautifully adorned with antique ornaments, tinsel, ribbons, bows, and sometimes edible items such as popcorn balls. Those that were within reach of Clipper sometimes disappeared without a trace. He loved to play and sniff around the tree, lending his noisy, energetic personality to the elegant decor. Luckily he never tried to knock it down.

When Mrs. Kennedy, Caroline, and John Jr. traveled on the *Caroline* for the official Christmas holiday in Palm Beach, Clipper and Charlie accompanied them on the plane and

The Kennedy and Radziwill families celebrate Christmas with Clipper and Charlie, Palm Beach, 1962. CECIL W. STOUGHTON, WHITE HOUSE PHOTOGRAPHS. JOHN F. KENNEDY PRESIDENTIAL LIBRARY AND MUSEUM.

were featured prominently in the family holiday photos. The Kennedy dogs were always considered an integral part of all family events, including all the Christmas festivities that year with Mrs. Kennedy's sister, Princess Lee Radziwill, and her family.

When the president arrived later at the Palm Beach airport, Clipper and Mrs. Kennedy were the first ones to greet him. Clipper was everywhere during that Christmas holiday. If he wasn't walking along the beach or swimming in the aqua blue waters, he was with the local police officers who were charged with protecting the presidential family, and was often mistaken for a police dog assigned to the Palm Beach Police Department.

One of the wonderful things about dogs is that they teach their owners great lessons in humility, and Clipper was no exception. When Italian Prime Minister Amintore Fanfani visited the White House in January 1963, he brought several gifts for the Kennedys, including a black-and-white stuffed animal that was presented to John Jr. Spying this new addition to the family's collection of toys, Clipper quickly made his move. Like a stealth bomber, he grabbed the stuffed animal and made a mad dash down the colonnade hall with his new prize gripped firmly between his jaws. Mrs. Kennedy chased him down to retrieve the toy, and the two engaged in a brief tug-of-war until the First Lady finally rescued the state gift, thereby avoiding an international incident.

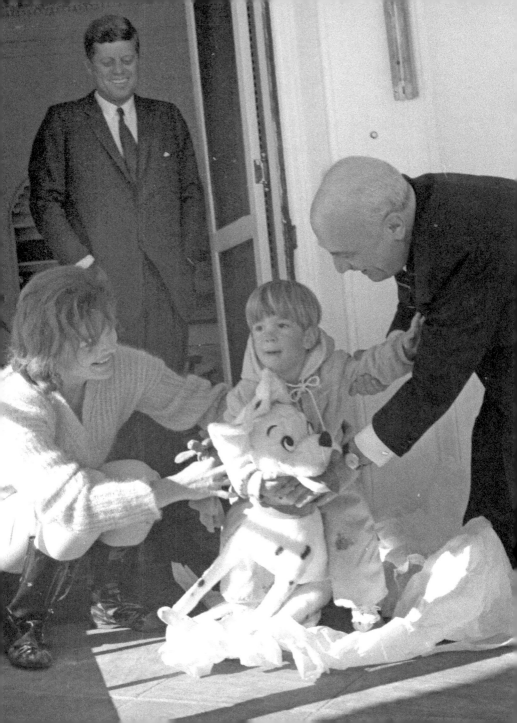

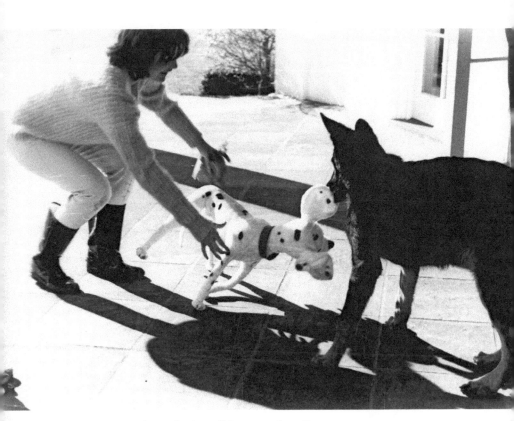

Mrs. Kennedy wrestles the stuffed toy away from Clipper. CECIL W. STOUGHTON, WHITE HOUSE PHOTOGRAPHS. JOHN F. KENNEDY PRESIDENTIAL LIBRARY AND MUSEUM.

Facing page: Mrs. Kennedy and Italian Prime Minister Amintore Fanfani give a stuffed toy dog to John Jr. in 1963, just before it was stolen away by Clipper. President Kennedy stands in the background. CECIL W. STOUGHTON, WHITE HOUSE PHOTOGRAPHS. JOHN F. KENNEDY PRESIDENTIAL LIBRARY AND MUSEUM.

Along with his playful personality, there was also the matter of his size. Clipper was a large, gangly pup, and Mrs. Kennedy was worried that he might grow up to be a menacingly large German Shepherd. In an attempt to avoid such a problem, she signed him up for obedience lessons through the Washington Metropolitan Police K9 training program.

Mrs. Kennedy and Caroline would watch the class, cheering Clipper on. He attended just four classes before having to drop out due to his increasing health problems. Police Lieutenant William Wright said that Clipper was an apt student, even though he certainly would not be class valedictorian.

What was never revealed to the public was the fact that Dr. Alan F. McEwan, the Kennedy's personal veterinarian, was quite concerned about Clipper being subjected to such a rigorous obedience training program. He offered several reasons why it was inadvisable to continue with the program: First, he felt that Clipper was too young for such intensive training. Second, he said that Clipper was very weak in the hindquarters (from the heart down) and could not endure too much jumping. And finally, he said he believed Clipper was not a "normal" German Shepherd and could not withstand such intensive training. He felt strongly that Clipper's training should be limited to companion dog training, which entails basic instructions such as "sit" and "heel," based on American Kennel Club guidelines.

Mrs. Kennedy pulls John Jr. on a sled on the South Lawn of the White House, while Clipper runs along with them, in 1962. CECIL W. STOUGHTON, WHITE HOUSE PHOTOGRAPHS. JOHN F. KENNEDY PRESIDENTIAL LIBRARY AND MUSEUM.

From Clipper's medical records, it was evident that he was often ill and required many supplements and veterinarian-prescribed diets to maintain his weight and health. Mrs.

Clipper – Jan. 16, 1963     P.T. Moran
         Copies – SS         ↗ M St.
              Sturrow
              Williams

morning: – 4 cups purina Kibbles.
          ¾ can Quaker city beef.
noon: –    same
night –    same.
Add: 1 Tsp. cooked bone meal in one of feedings
If possible, a cup of cooked rice added to the
night meal would help (this, in addition to the
Kibbles + beef.)
        I noticed you have some Vi-supple-min.
this could be used daily also (Tablespoon added to
one of the meals per day.) sorb
   The milk bone biscuits can be used as Treats
or given when Clipper is put away for the night.
        I could find no fleas on clipper but his coat
is dry + this would probably account for his
continued scratching. He could be bathed with the
flea oil shampoo once a week. Paul (one of my
kennel boys) would be glad to do this down     OK
here if you wish. Paul grooms your mother's
poodle (Charlie.) This dry coat will improve as time goes
on – it is actually associated with the very poor start
clipper had – actually I think he is doing
very well.

A note from veterinarian Dr. Alan F. McEwan about Clipper's health issues and recommended diet in 1963. JACQUELINE BOUVIER KENNEDY ONASSIS PERSONAL PAPERS. JOHN F. KENNEDY PRESIDENTIAL LIBRARY AND MUSEUM.

Kennedy personally supervised his medical needs to be sure he stayed in tip-top health.

As Mrs. Kennedy's companion, Clipper was often allowed upstairs in the family quarters when the president was traveling or working in the West Wing. He was also a frequent flier on Air Force One, Marine One, and the *Caroline*. He was a good traveler and would typically curl up at the feet of his beloved owner. She was seldom without him when she spent her weekends at the family home in Atoka, Virginia.

Although Clipper was basically fearless by nature, early in his travel career he had been startled by the thundering sound of Marine One's rotor blades as they descended upon the great lawn in Hyannis Port. This made him so anxious that he crashed right through a closed screen door. Eventually, however, he learned to travel on Marine One without incident, and was always welcome on the military aircraft.

During the Kennedy White House years, the Kennedy Compound in Hyannis Port was a place for the family to have fun and unwind with touch football games, swimming, golf, tennis, and their pets. Caroline and John Jr., along with other Kennedy, Shriver, and Lawford children, were frequently driven around in a golf cart named the "Toonerville Trolley" to places such as their favorite candy store. In an off-the-record incident on one of these trips, Secret Service agent Bob Foster accidentally ran over Clipper. The accident

Mrs. Kennedy with President Kennedy and her beloved Clipper at Atoka in 1963.
COLLECTION. JOHN F. KENNEDY PRESIDENTIAL LIBRARY AND MUSEUM.

fractured Clipper's olecranon process, otherwise known as the bony protrusion of the elbow, on one of his legs. Foster was distraught about the accident, but both President and Mrs. Kennedy attempted to put him at ease.

Dr. Arthur Bernstein, a young veterinarian on Cape Cod, remembered the day the president called him to speak with him about the injury and treatment. He said it was "a distinctive voice I shall never forget." Having just graduated from veterinary school the year before, Dr. Bernstein was not keen on performing such a complicated procedure on the First Family's dog. Eventually the Kennedys decided to send Clipper to the military vets in Washington, DC, who had a lot more experience with this type of injury, and Dr. Bernstein was greatly relieved. Clipper recovered quickly from the procedure and was soon accompanying Mrs. Kennedy on their nightly walks once again.

The president himself took a very active role in the care of his cherished canines. "Every time he [the president] would see me he would ask me questions about the dogs' health, if they were giving me a hard time, or if they were eating well," kennel keeper Traphes Bryant said in an interview with the John F. Kennedy Presidential Library. "Sometimes I saw him once a day."

In his book, *Dog Days at the White House*, Bryant explains that at some point President Kennedy didn't want him to

November 24, 1962
12:00 Noon

Mrs. Kennedy,

The following is the menu that Dr. Bernstein recommends for Clipper. It is a special diet that is supposed to help the condition causing the loose stool.

## Morning

1/3 can of I.D.     plus Vitamin drops directly in mouth and   (Only once a
1/3 can of P.D.     Mineral powders sprinkled on food     day on Vitamins
Hot Water and Kibble Kennel Biscuits             & Minerals)

## Noon

Same as above minus Vitamins and Minerals

## Night

Same as above minus Vitamins and Minerals
Cottage Cheese or Cooked (Scrambled) egg or Hamburger (cooked or raw)

Dr. Bernstein recommends no whole milk for now. It would be alright to mix some milk powder in the food.

Dr. Bernstein says Clipper's stool should be watched closely - checked every day for time being. He recommends that Clipper be checked by a Vet in Washington once a week.

Dr. Bernstein checked Clipper's front legs and is of the opinion that there is nothing seriously wrong. He feels the limp will improve shortly and is the result of the dog's age and growing pains. He thinks maybe it could be a tender shoulder muscle that could have been strained through jumping. In other words the doctor didn't seem very concerned about the limp and believes it will correct itself in time.

*Lynn Meredith*
Lynn Meredith

I obtained from Dr. Bernstein the following items:

1 box of I.D. Dog Food
1 box of P.D. Dog Food
1 50 lb. bag of Kibble Kennel Biscuits
1 small bottle of liquid Vitamins
2 bottles of minerals in powder form

Both Clipper and Charlie received the necessary shot injection.

**Dr. Arthur Bernstein's suggested diet for Clipper in 1962.** JACQUELINE BOUVIER KENNEDY ONASSIS PERSONAL PAPERS. JOHN F. KENNEDY PRESIDENTIAL LIBRARY AND MUSEUM.

throw any more balls or sticks to Clipper and issued the same order to the Secret Service. Bryant was puzzled by this because President Kennedy always loved to see his dogs perform tricks. He soon learned that the reason was because Clipper would lunge for the club whenever President Kennedy practiced his golf swing. In one instance, this nearly dislocated the president's shoulder. Other times, he'd end up swinging the club with Clipper attached.

Bryant had trained the dogs to greet the president in an extraordinary way. Whenever President Kennedy emerged from his helicopter on the White House lawn, his dogs would line up to pay their respects, like a reception of distinguished heads of state. The president would break into a broad grin, go through the line, and salute and pat each canine. Clipper in particular provided the president not only with respect but with the opportunity to impart his love of animals to his children. Once, when the president saw John Jr. pulling Clipper's tail, he gently instructed him not to do it because "dogs are our friends." John Jr. would grow up to become an ardent dog lover himself.

On rare occasions, President Kennedy and Charlie would join Mrs. Kennedy and Clipper on their early evening walk around the White House grounds. The First Couple would escape with their favorite companions—leaving behind, if only briefly, the stresses of White House life. Bryant remembered a night when the pair walked the dogs under a hard,

Evelyn Lincoln, personal secretary to President Kennedy, with Clipper in the Oval office in 1962. CECIL W. STOUGHTON, WHITE HOUSE PHOTOGRAPHS. JOHN F. KENNEDY PRESIDENTIAL LIBRARY AND MUSEUM.

Mrs. Kennedy with John Jr. and Clipper after sledding, walking toward President Kennedy on the White House grounds, in 1962. CECIL W. STOUGHTON, WHITE HOUSE PHOTOGRAPHS. JOHN F. KENNEDY PRESIDENTIAL LIBRARY AND MUSEUM.

cold rain, and the president wasn't wearing a hat. To Bryant the president and Mrs. Kennedy looked flushed and happy when they returned, like "two young college kids taking the dogs for a walk."

During an interview with Nancy Tuckerman and Pamela Turnure for the John F. Kennedy Presidential Library, White House usher J. B. West recalled an unexpected moment with Mrs. Kennedy during her historic renovation of the Blue Room, one of three state parlors on the first floor of White House. Before the room was opened to the public, Mrs. Kennedy wanted to meet with Stephane Boudin, the chief designer of the project, for last-minute changes. West said, "We stopped the tourists for a period of time so that she [Mrs. Kennedy] could come through, and when she got off the elevator, she said, 'I think I'd like to go out and take a walk first. Can I come in later?' . . . So I said, 'Certainly, go ahead.' And I let the tourists go on. [I said to Mrs. Kennedy,] 'You can come in through the door off the porch.'"

After returning from their walk, Mrs. Kennedy and Clipper surprised West by "climbing through the window into the Blue Room with muddy feet in the white-walled room."

Despite Clipper's close bond with Mrs. Kennedy, the *Washington Post* ran a tongue-in-cheek story on May 15, 1963, about his low "prestige rating" on his dog license. This rating is based on who owns the dog, with the most prominent owners

Ben Bradlee (then editor of the *Washington Post*), Toni Bradlee, Mrs. Kennedy, Clipper, President Kennedy, and family friend Paul Fout at Atoka in 1963.
CECIL W. STOUGHTON, WHITE HOUSE PHOTOGRAPHS. JOHN F. KENNEDY PRESIDENTIAL LIBRARY AND MUSEUM.

receiving the lowest dog license numbers. The article was titled "Prestige Is Going to the Dogs in the Nation's Capitol," and it quoted John Nelson, assistant chief of the District of Columbia licensing bureau, as saying:

*Yesterday, President Kennedy's three dogs will be given
the lowest number prestige of 1, 2, 3 on their licenses
this year. "Charlie," the Welsh Terrier belonging to the
Kennedy family, has been the number one dog in town
for more than a year. But "Pushinka," a gift from
Soviet Prime Minister Khrushchev, and "Clipper,"
the family's German shepherd, have been relegated to
the fairly low status of numbers 9 and 10. This new
line up meant downgrading for some of the canine
licenses of two other well-known names, Vice President
Johnson's Beagle will drop from 2 to 4, FBI Director J.
Edgar Hoover's two Cairn Terrier dogs will slip from
3-4 to 5-6.*

Oblivious to his low prestige number, Clipper enjoyed his
days at the White House and on the Cape. Here on the wide
lawn of Ambassador Kennedy's oceanfront home, he was able
to fully indulge his compulsive ball chasing. He made sure he
was heard loudly, even above the din of Hyannis Port, and
enjoyed the consumption of many of the Kennedy children's
stuffed animals.

White House photographer Cecil B. Stoughton captured
many images of Clipper. For example, he shot the famous
canine at the Kennedys' Atoka, Virginia, estate as Clipper followed the golf cart in which Mrs. Kennedy was riding, never

President Kennedy feeds Clipper on the White House grounds in 1963, while Maud Shaw, nanny to Caroline and John Jr., looks on. CECIL W. STOUGHTON, WHITE HOUSE PHOTOGRAPHS. JOHN F. KENNEDY PRESIDENTIAL LIBRARY AND MUSEUM.

leaving her side. Clipper was also shown walking with John Jr. and his nanny Maud Shaw, visiting the horses in the stable along with the president, Ben and Toni Bradlee, and Paul Fout.

The last time Bryant saw President Kennedy was on the evening of November 20, 1963, before he went to Dallas. Dressed in his bathrobe, the president was fresh from a swim in the pool, and the two discussed Clipper's feud with Wolf, the Irish Wolfhound that was part of the Kennedy K-9 corps.

Bryant explained that Clipper had been picking on Wolf, but Wolf was growing up fast and learning to retaliate. He then assured the president that he would do his best to stop the fighting. The president informed Bryant that Charlie had snapped at John Jr. in the president's office, and Bryant promised he would take care of this as well. President Kennedy graciously thanked him and went into the mansion to change his clothes for the evening meal. Bryant never saw him again.

According to Secret Service agent Clint Hill, Mrs. Kennedy and her children remained in the White House for about two weeks after the tragedy in Dallas. Before Mrs. Kennedy left, she was forced to make some difficult decisions regarding the family dogs. Clipper was sent to live with the Kennedy family's good friends, Paul and Eve Fout, of Middleburg, Virginia. Paul Fout was a renowned, Eclipse Award–winning horseman and responsible for the care of the Kennedy family horses. Eve

Prime Fout was a gifted horsewoman and artist and was the favored riding companion of Mrs. Kennedy. The Fouts had three children, Virginia, Nina, and Doug.

Although Clipper was recognized as a strong-willed dog, he slept in Doug's room and grew to be quite protective of him. He was also wary of strangers but was extremely loyal to those he trusted—continuing to fulfill Ambassador Kennedy's expectation. On the occasions when Mrs. Kennedy would come to Middleburg, Virginia, and ride with Mrs. Fout, Clipper would bound toward her as if she had just returned from a state trip.

He would never forget his first lady, and always enjoyed their reunions.

Mrs. Kennedy also played a leading role in the story of another canine with an outsize personality—a dog named Pushinka.

Pushinka in front of the White House in 1962. ROBERT L. KNUDSEN, WHITE HOUSE PHOTOGRAPHS. JOHN F. KENNEDY PRESIDENTIAL LIBRARY AND MUSEUM.

## Chapter Four

# The Soviet Space Dog and a Cold War Romance

This is the story of a famous romance that seemed to bridge the divide between the US and the USSR during the height of the Cold War. It started with a little white dog named Pushinka.

Pushinka's saga at the White House can be traced to June 1961, when President John F. Kennedy and Soviet Premier Nikita Khrushchev met in Vienna, Austria. Tensions between the two nations were escalating and would soon be pushed to the brink with the Cuban missile crisis, which was less than one year away. The Berlin Wall was in the process of being built. Photographs of the talks between the two world leaders at this time capture the strain and acrimony in their expressions.

By contrast, at a state dinner given by Austrian President Adolf Schärf at the Schöenbrunn Palace in Vienna, the photos show a smiling Mrs. Kennedy, dressed in a glimmering gown and her trademark long-sleeved gloves, sitting beside a laughing and visibly delighted Khrushchev. According to an interview with Mrs. Kennedy by historian Arthur Schlesinger, in his book *A Thousand Days*, the First Lady "remarked to Krushchev that she had read that one of the Soviet dogs that had gone into space had recently given birth—and jokingly said to Khrushchev, 'Why don't you send me one?'"

A few days after the Kennedys flew back to Washington, they received a rather startling visit from Soviet Ambassador Mikhail Menshikov. He was carrying in his arms a small white puppy named Pushinka (Russian for "little bit of fluff"), who was clearly terrified.

"How did this dog get here?" asked a bewildered President Kennedy, according to the Kennedy Library transcript.

"I'm afraid I asked Khrushchev for it in Vienna when I was running out of things to say," Mrs. Kennedy replied. Along with Pushinka, Premier Khrushchev also sent some other gifts, including a photo album of Moscow, liqueur, nine bottles of perfume, and a golden tea set.

Note from Evelyn Lincoln in 1961 about letters regarding Pushinka, who is referred to as "fluff" because *pushinka* is Russian for "bit of fluff." JACQUELINE BOUVIER KENNEDY ONASSIS PERSONAL PAPERS. JOHN F. KENNEDY PRESIDENTIAL LIBRARY AND MUSEUM.

Pushinka, described as "nervous and high-strung," was the offspring of a female dog named Strelka (Russian for "arrow"), who rocketed into space on August 19, 1960, aboard *Sputnik V*, and a male dog named Pushok (loosely translated as "fluffy white kitten"), who was part of the space program but never went into orbit. The Russians were experimenting with dogs in space to determine if conditions were feasible for humans.

Dogs were chosen because Russian scientists believed canines would be able to endure the long stretches of inactivity in space. To prepare for the flights, they were confined in tiny boxes for fifteen to twenty days at a stretch. They were

**Pushinka's passport.** JACQUELINE BOUVIER KENNEDY ONASSIS PERSONAL PAPERS.
JOHN F. KENNEDY PRESIDENTIAL LIBRARY AND MUSEUM.

Pushinka (center) with her space dog mother, Strelka (left), and her father, Pushok (right), in Russia in 1961. COLLECTION. JOHN F. KENNEDY PRESIDENTIAL LIBRARY AND MUSEUM.

also placed in rocket launch simulators wearing space suits and were fed a nutritious jelly-like protein.

Strelka proved to be the most intrepid of the approximately sixty Russian space dogs. She made history when she became the first earthborn creature to survive a twenty-one-hour spaceflight, with sixteen orbits around the earth. Accompanying her were another dog, a rabbit, forty-two mice, two rats, flies, and a number of plants and fungi. After her successful flight, Strelka achieved instant fame in the Soviet Union. On December 30, 1960, she gave birth to a litter of six puppies, including Pushinka, who spent most of their early years in a laboratory with their famous mother.

Was President Kennedy skeptical of Khrushchev's intentions, thinking that such a gift might symbolize Russia's superior position in the space race? Maybe so, but Pushinka's arrival at the White House at the height of the Cold War certainly aroused the suspicions of the CIA, who thought she might have been implanted with listening devices. The tiny puppy was taken to the Walter Reed Army Hospital, where she was poked, prodded, x-rayed, scanned with a magnetometer, and even subjected to an early version of a sonogram. The official spin in *Time* magazine was that she had suffered a "nervous breakdown" on the long, intercontinental flight. In an interview conducted on September 15, 2011, on *The Daily Show with Jon Stewart*, Caroline Kennedy remembered Pushinka as a "nervous dog who bit everyone" and created quite a stir. The family attributed Pushinka's overwrought behavior to her laboratory upbringing.

There was one particular instance when Caroline and her nanny, Maud Shaw, encountered Pushinka with White House kennel keeper Bryant. As Caroline reached forward to pet the fluffy white dog, she growled. Instead of backing away, Caroline walked behind the dog and gave her a kick in the rear end. When Miss Shaw told this story to President Kennedy, he grinned at his daughter and said, "That's giving it to those damn Russians!"

| INSTRUCTIONS | | |
|---|---|---|
| **DOG TAGS FOR ALL DOGS WILL EXPIRE ON JUNE 30th.**<br>• IF YOU NO LONGER HAVE THE DOG DESCRIBED ON I LL YOU MAY USE THI FORM TO APPLY FOR A TAG FOR ANOTHER DOG. THE CHANGED DESCRIPTION MUST BE MADE ON BOTH SIDES OF TI S FORM. ONLY ONE TAG MAY BE APPLIED FOR ON THIS FORM.<br><br>• MAIL BOTH THIS APPLICATION AND THE ATTACHED BILL WITH $3.00 IN CHECK OR MONEY ORDER ONLY TO: LICENSE BRANCH, DEPARTMENT OF LICENSES AND INSPECTIONS, WASHINGTON 4, D.C. THIS APPLICATION MUST BE RECEIVED BY JUNE 30TH.<br><br>• MAKE C^ECK OR MONEY ORDER PAYABLE TO: D.C. TREASURER.<br><br>• THE DOG TAG WILL BE MAILED TO YOU. | **IMPORTANT:** THIS TAG HAS BEEN ISSUED AFTER IT IS NOT TRANSFERRABLE | Commissioners Order No. 61-1734<br>Police Regulations Article 18, Section 2 as amended:<br><br>"No animal of the dog kind shall be allowed to go at large without a collar or tag, as now prescribed by law, and no person owning, keeping or having custody of a dog in the District shall permit such dog to be on any public space in the District, unless such dog is firmly secured by a substantial leash, not exceeding four feet in length, held by a person capable of managing such dog, nor shall any dog be permitted to go on private property without the consent of the owner or occupant thereof." |

Instructions for Pushinka's dog tags in 1962. JACQUELINE BOUVIER KENNEDY ONASSIS PERSONAL PAPERS. JOHN F. KENNEDY PRESIDENTIAL LIBRARY AND MUSEUM.

Despite her nervous nature, Pushinka was also a highly intelligent dog, perhaps due to her stellar lineage. She proved this when she learned from Bryant how to climb the ladder of Caroline's tree house, walk across the platform, and slide down the chute on the other side.

According to *Dog Days at the White House*, when President Kennedy saw Pushinka gliding down the chute, he reportedly asked Bryant, "How in the world did you ever get a dog to do that?" Bryant showed the president the peanut in his hand and replied, "No problem, Mr. President. I just move a peanut up the ladder one step at a time and Pushinka follows the peanut. She'll do anything for a peanut. She also knows that there is a peanut at the bottom of the slide." As the president shook his head in amazement, his astute political instincts kicked in. "That's worth six million votes right there," he said,

and asked Bryant to have some photos taken of the Russian dog's slide trick, which made their way into press reports.

This trick etched itself indelibly into the memory of John F. Kennedy Jr. In fact, in a CNN interview with Larry King on September 28, 1995, John Jr. recalled that watching Pushinka's slide trick was his earliest, and perhaps only, recollection of his days at the White House.

Pushinka's celebrity status with the American public continued to grow. On August 23, 1961, the millionth visitor to the White House that year was Mrs. Edith Sprayberry of Rome, Georgia, who with her husband and three children was given a tour of the Oval Office by President Kennedy. She also received an autographed picture of him, along with one of Pushinka.

On December 5, 1961, the Kennedys had a scare when Pushinka was briefly lost after slipping through the iron gates at the White House. After the dog was found, Mrs. Kennedy instructed the maintenance staff to place chicken wire over the gates to prevent further escapes and paint it black, but it was soon removed because tourists were pulling it down. Mrs. Kennedy also found it aesthetically unappealing.

Facing page: The ending of Pushinka's slide trick, on the South Lawn of the White House in 1962. John Jr. would later say this trick was his only memory of his White House years. CECIL W. STOUGHTON, WHITE HOUSE PHOTOGRAPHS. JOHN F. KENNEDY PRESIDENTIAL LIBRARY AND MUSEUM.

Meanwhile, romance was blossoming between Pushinka and Charlie, the president's Welsh Terrier. At this time, tensions between the US and the USSR had continued to escalate and reached their peak during the Cuban missile crisis in October 1962. In his book, *Dog Days at the White House*, Bryant wrote, "It is tempting to speculate that during this time, when the President held the world's fate in his hands, he thought about these animals, companionable together and blissfully unaware of potential nuclear annihilation. Or perhaps the First Lady, an important confidante to the president and a shrewd judge of psychology, spoke of the human motivations of the Soviets, including Chairman Khrushchev who had given her a dog as a personal gift."

Pushinka made headlines again after she and Charlie had four puppies on June 14, 1963. Newspapers throughout the country reported on the birth, which was also a matter of great interest to President Kennedy. When Pushinka was pregnant, he reportedly checked on her condition daily. On one of his daily visits, he noticed that Bryant had placed a copy of the pro-Republican *New York Tribune* in Pushinka's litter box. When President Kennedy saw this, he laughed and said, "It's finally found its proper use."

After the birth of the puppies, which he referred to as "pupniks," the president was equally concerned with their

Charlie, Clipper, and Pushinka play together on the White House lawn in 1963.
CECIL W. STOUGHTON, WHITE HOUSE PHOTOGRAPHS, JOHN F. KENNEDY PRESIDENTIAL LIBRARY AND MUSEUM.

Charlie and Pushinka sit companionably in front of the White House in 1962.
ROBERT L. KNUDSEN, WHITE HOUSE PHOTOGRAPHS. JOHN F. KENNEDY PRESIDENTIAL
LIBRARY AND MUSEUM.

Facing page: Charlie and Pushinka on the White House lawn with Robert M.
Redmond, chief White House gardener, and White House staffer Hassel Adams
in 1961. ROBERT L. KNUDSEN, WHITE HOUSE PHOTOGRAPHS. JOHN F. KENNEDY
PRESIDENTIAL LIBRARY AND MUSEUM.

welfare. The puppies included two males, Streaker and Blackie, and two females, Butterfly and White Tips.

At this time, Mrs. Kennedy was pregnant with her third child, and the president orchestrated a surprise for Caroline and John as they awaited the birth of their new brother or sister in a gray-shingled rented home called Brambletyde on Squaw Island in Cape Cod. On August 2, 1963, President Kennedy asked Bryant to fly Pushinka and her puppies from the White House to Brambletyde.

When they arrived, the dogs and Bryant were hidden in the US Secret Service trailer until President Kennedy called for them. Bryant later recalled the outburst of joy from the children as they saw the dogs, who were soon "roaming happily around the lawn."

Not long after, Mrs. Kennedy was rushed by helicopter to Otis Air Force Base hospital, where a very ill, premature baby boy, Patrick Bouvier Kennedy, was delivered by Cesarean section on August 7. He weighed only four pounds five ounces and would live for less than two days. Sadly, Patrick died on August 9, 1963.

While recovering from this tragedy, Mrs. Kennedy learned that more than five thousand letters were being sent to the White House requesting Pushinka's puppies, and she decided to give them away through a contest based on the letters.

Two of the four puppies of Charlie and Pushinka, the offspring of a Cold War romance. COLLECTION. JOHN F. KENNEDY PRESIDENTIAL LIBRARY AND MUSEUM.

In a note to White House secretary Pam Turnure, Mrs. Kennedy wrote:

*Pam:*

*I read a story where we got 5,000 letters, asking for one of the puppies. Would you have someone go through them and pick out a few likely candidates, without telling anyone we are doing this. I would like to give one of the puppies to some child, who is really deserving, who has never had a dog, or who is sick, etc. But, of course, we will have someone check on the family first to make sure the child doesn't have a drunken father, who would smash the dog against the wall, etc. So would you have some one look through the letters for a really sweet child and, as soon as you find a few, bring them to my attention.*

*Thanks, J.*

Mrs. Kennedy also requested that Turnure ask the family of Vice President Lyndon Johnson if they would like a puppy, in the following letter:

*One thought about the puppies, which you might want to consider: As you know, the Johnsons were devoted to their "Little Beagle Johnson," who was stolen or died several months ago, so perhaps you might want to give a puppy to them to take his place.*

President Kennedy with Caroline as she plays with one of Pushinka's puppies on the family yacht, the *Honey Fitz*, in 1963. Mrs. Kennedy would later launch a children's letter-writing contest in which the puppies were awarded as the prizes. CECIL W. STOUGHTON, WHITE HOUSE PHOTOGRAPHS. JOHN F. KENNEDY PRESIDENTIAL LIBRARY AND MUSEUM.

Caroline with one of Pushinka's puppies on Cape Cod in 1963. John Jr. is in the background. CECIL W. STOUGHTON, WHITE HOUSE PHOTOGRAPHS. JOHN F. KENNEDY PRESIDENTIAL LIBRARY AND MUSEUM.

However, the Johnsons declined Mrs. Kennedy's offer. She set to work on her contest with the children's letters, and by the time she left the Otis Air Force Base hospital, she was narrowing down her search.

Mrs. Kennedy eventually selected ten-year-old Karen House of Westchester, Illinois, as the winner of the puppy named Butterfly based on this letter:

*Dear Mr. President,*
*I would like to have one of your pretty dog puppies. I would like a puppy so much because I never had a dog before and I like yours very much.*
*If you give me a puppy I will be so happy.*
*PS Write me back and answer my letter please Mr. Kennedy I don't know how to spell the name of the dog who just had babies.*
*Sincerely yours,*
*Karen E. House*

The winner of the pup named Streaker was nine-year-old Mark Bruce of Columbia, Missouri. His letter read:

*Dear Mrs. Kennedy,*
*The other day I heard on the radio that the dog Mr. Khrushchev gave to you had pups and you didn't know what to do with them.*

White House electrician and kennel keeper Traphes Bryant with Pushinka and her puppies on the White House lawn in 1963. The four puppies, Butterfly, White Tips, Blackie, and Streaker, were sired by Charlie. CECIL W. STOUGHTON, WHITE HOUSE PHOTOGRAPHS. JOHN F. KENNEDY PRESIDENTIAL LIBRARY AND MUSEUM.

*On June 8th I was playing baseball I was batting and our dog Midget got behind me when swinging the bat and I accidently [sic] hit her in the head. She died almost immediately. I'm a member of the Parkdale 4-H Midget was my project. I was in dog care. If you would let me have one of the pups I could continue in 4-H. The transportation may be a problem. My Dad and brothers and a few other boys will be going to Washington DC for the National RA Congress. If you will let us have it they could pick it up.*

The president's secretary, Evelyn Norton Lincoln, informed the winners of the good news on August 18, 1963, by phone. Karen E. House received Butterfly at O'Hare Airport in Chicago, and on August 20, Mark Bruce was presented with Streaker at Columbia Airport in Missouri.

As for Pushinka's other "pupniks," they remained at Squaw Island until President Kennedy was assassinated. Blackie was then given to President Kennedy's sister Pat and her husband, Peter Lawford, while White Tips went to Kennedy nurse Luella Hennessey, who took care of the Kennedy women when they were pregnant.

Pushinka herself went to live with White House gardener Irvin Williams and his family in Vienna, Virginia, after the Kennedys left the White House. "Mrs. Kennedy had asked me if I wanted to take her, and I agreed," said Williams in

John Jr. with one of Pushinka's puppies on Cape Cod in 1963. CECIL W. STOUGHTON, WHITE HOUSE PHOTOGRAPHS. JOHN F. KENNEDY PRESIDENTIAL LIBRARY AND MUSEUM.

Facing page: Caroline with one of Pushinka's puppies on the *Honey Fitz* at Cape Cod in 1963. CECIL W. STOUGHTON, WHITE HOUSE PHOTOGRAPHS. JOHN F. KENNEDY PRESIDENTIAL LIBRARY AND MUSEUM.

a recent interview. "Mrs. Kennedy knew how much I loved Pushinka. I loved the Kennedy years. It was an exciting time, filled with dogs and children. They were a great family."

To Williams, Pushinka, was a special favorite. "Pushinka was always in my office," he says. "She was my shadow."

He recalled the "terrible day" of November 22, 1963, when President Kennedy was shot. "I went with the military to work on the grave site, to help plant shrubs, do the landscaping, hook up the eternal torch to the gas. I brought Pushinka," he said. "It was a very sad day."

Williams described Pushinka as a "shy" dog, but very affectionate and beloved by his family. His home has three acres, so she had "lots of room to run," he said.

Perhaps harking back to her mother's famous space travels, Pushinka loved to take trips and ride in the car. "She was also very smart," Irvin said. "We would take her on vacation trips to Massachusetts and when we were getting close to home, she seemed to know, and would sit up, with her paws on the dashboard."

# Chapter Five

# The White House Menagerie

Along with their dogs, the animal-loving Kennedy family brought a colorful menagerie of other pets to the White House. The animals included Tom Kitten, a mischievous cat; Zsa Zsa, a beer-drinking rabbit that could play the trumpet; Debbie and Billie, two troublesome hamsters; Robin, a canary; and Bluebelle and Maybelle, two parakeets. These pets seemed to provide a constant source of comic relief at the Kennedy White House. From Tom Kitten's regal but short-lived stay in the presidential living quarters to the birds that perched on the president's head and the hamsters that hid in his bed and bathtub, their antics became a running narrative in the press.

Tom Kitten was the first feline to live at the White House since Teddy Roosevelt's cats, Tom Quartz and Slippers. A diminutive gray cat with yellow eyes, Tom Kitten was given to Caroline in the summer of 1959 by Mary Pinchot Meyer, the sister of Toni Bradlee, who was married to Benjamin Bradlee, the *Washington Post*'s executive editor. Toni Bradlee would later become John Jr.'s godmother.

Like Charlie the Welsh Terrier, Tom Kitten had first lived with the Kennedys at their Georgetown home. After the birth of John Jr. on November 25, 1960, Mrs. Kennedy went to Palm Beach for a brief vacation with Caroline and the new baby, and asked her mother and stepfather, Janet and Hugh Auchincloss, to take care of Tom Kitten at Merrywood, their McLean, Virginia, estate. Tom Kitten did not adapt well to his temporary living quarters, and Mrs. Auchincloss called the president-elect to discuss the cat's unruly behavior. The butler told her that her son-in-law was in the middle of an important meeting, but Mrs. Auchincloss insisted on speaking with him. When he came to the phone, she informed him that Tom Kitten was clawing her grand piano and starting fights with her dog. The cat was wreaking havoc and had to go, she said.

The president-elect then called Toni Bradlee and asked for her help. She sought the assistance of Kenneth Crawford, a *Newsweek* magazine editor who had recently lost a Poodle. He agreed to babysit the cat, and Tom Kitten was sent to

Mrs. Kennedy's press secretary, Pamela Turnure, holds Tom Kitten at a press conference on January 24, 1961. ABBIE ROWE, WHITE HOUSE PHOTOGRAPHS. JOHN F. KENNEDY PRESIDENTIAL LIBRARY AND MUSEUM.

the Crawford home in Georgetown. This arrangement was marked by a visit to the vet and a three-day escape that resulted in Tom Kitten being picked up by the Georgetown police.

Unchastened by the episode, Tom Kitten then scratched Crawford's two-year-old granddaughter in the face after she pulled his tail.

Once again, Tom Kitten was ignominiously asked to leave, but this time he was sent by limousine to the White House. At first, the feline was not pleased. He explored the historic family living quarters and "began meowing loudly," according to Mary Gallagher, Mrs. Kennedy's personal secretary. Soon afterward, he began to adapt to his new home, and Mrs. Kennedy wrote a thank-you note to Kenneth Crawford, saying that Tom Kitten was sleeping on the "Queen's bed" at the White House and that George, the butler, was taking care of him.

Like the Kennedy dogs, Tom Kitten soon made a splash in the media. On January 24, 1961 he was introduced to the White House Press Corps when he arrived at the briefing room with deputy press secretary Andrew Thomas Hatcher and Pamela Turnure, press secretary to Jacqueline Kennedy. The flurry of questions that erupted was fielded by Pierre Salinger, President Kennedy's press liaison. Soon, Salinger was issuing daily briefings on Tom Kitten's behavior, as the head-strong feline settled into life at the White House.

But the cat's presence exacerbated the president's allergies, which were less severely triggered by dogs. In the book *Sweet Caroline* by Christopher Andersen, Mrs. Kennedy recalled how the president "found it difficult to breathe" when Tom

Kitten was around. According to her oral history provided to the JFK Library, the president's mother-in-law, Janet Auchincloss, believed his allergy to animals "only started after his experience in the Pacific. I think it had something to do with it. And all those days on an atoll with nothing but coconut milk or whatever they lived on may have started this, and all the sickness he had after it, because I've been told that as a boy he could have dogs."

The allergy caused his eyes to become "all puffed and swollen." Mrs. Auchincloss remembered that the president would try to alleviate the problem by using "whatever spray he had to use to try to get himself breathing again." He didn't let the allergy stop him from keeping his beloved dogs, but the addition of a cat proved too difficult.

Mrs. Kennedy asked Mary Gallagher to adopt Tom Kitten, and she agreed. When Mrs. Kennedy explained the problem to Caroline, "she was very understanding and didn't make a fuss at all," Mrs. Kennedy related to Andersen. "She loved Tom Kitten, but when we explained how sick he made Daddy, she understood completely."

After thirty-six days of White House life, Tom Kitten departed in a basket to the Gallagher residence in Alexandria, Virginia. Salinger announced the news to the press corps, adding that Gallagher's two sons, Christopher, age four, and Gregory, age three, had already given the cat a new name.

The new moniker came when Mrs. Gallagher had attempted to introduce the cat to her boys, saying, "This is Tom . . ." But before she could finish, the boys chimed in with "Tom Terrific," based on a character from the *Captain Kangaroo* television show.

Caroline Kennedy missed her cat and made three visits to the Gallagher home to see him. The first visit took place in April 1961, when Caroline, accompanied by her nanny, Maud Shaw, and Secret Service agents Robert Foster and Lynn Meredith, stayed for three hours to play with Tom Kitten.

The following year, in March, Caroline once again arrived at the Gallagher home to see Tom Kitten, this time with her mother and brother and several more Secret Service agents. On this occasion, they had tea, and Tom Kitten sat at the table with Caroline, who reportedly fed him chicken and laughed when he licked her fingers. Caroline's final visit to see her cat took place in June 1962, when she went with a friend, Agatha Pozen, to the Gallagher home, along with the usual coterie of Secret Service agents. The group took Tom Kitten for a picnic of hot dogs, hamburgers, and milk shakes along the nearby riverbank.

Caroline received the sad news from the Gallaghers about Tom Kitten's death on August 21, 1962, while she was on a trip to Italy with her mother. When she returned home, Caroline went to the Gallaghers' home to pay her final respects.

Caroline holds a cat in Evelyn Lincoln's White House office in 1963.
CECIL W. STOUGHTON, WHITE HOUSE PHOTOGRAPHS. JOHN F. KENNEDY
PRESIDENTIAL LIBRARY AND MUSEUM.

Tom Kitten's obituary was published in the *Alexandria Gazette*, with this report: "Unlike many humans in the same position, he never wrote his memoirs of his days at the White House or with the Kennedys, he never discussed them for quotation though he was privy to many official secrets."

Another pet who was the subject of Pierre Salinger's White House briefings was a chubby white rabbit named Zsa Zsa. In his book *With Kennedy*, Salinger recounted, "Zsa Zsa was a beer-swilling, trumpet-tooting rabbit who was given to Caroline by Pittsburgh magician Harry Albacker." In one of his exchanges with the press, Salinger was asked, "Mr. Secretary, do you know that this rabbit is a lush?" He replied, "All I know about Zsa Zsa is that she is supposed to be able to play the first five bars of the 'The Star-Spangled Banner' on a golden toy trumpet."

The trouble-prone hamsters, Debbie and Billie, were given to Caroline by Teddy Smith of Rye Brook, New York, whose father worked with Lem Billings, according to an interview with Evelyn Lincoln from the Kennedy Library. On their second night in the White House, the hamsters figured out how to escape from their cage, and President Kennedy found them in his bathroom. The next night, the president discovered the pair hiding under his bed.

The White House reporters found these episodes highly amusing, and Salinger described their keen interest in the two rodents: The most newsworthy inhabitants of the White House zoo were Caroline's hamsters. They were always running away, catching a cold, or planning their own demise in a way that would delight James Bond. The White House Press Corps, particularly the distaff reporters, took a lively interest in the health and welfare of the hamsters. According to Salinger:

> *Helen Thomas of UPI woke me out of a sound sleep one morning at three o'clock. "I wouldn't call you at an ungodly hour like this, Pierre, if it weren't important. But we have a report that one of Caroline's hamsters has died. Will you check it out for me?" I exploded. "Who would you like me to call, Helen? Caroline? Mrs. Kennedy? The President himself?"*

In March 1961 the *Chicago Tribune* ran a story titled "Caroline Runs Hamster Hunt in White House: Staff Helps Search for Her Two Lost Pets." The article described the hamsters' penchant for escaping their cage and roaming the historic halls while the White House staff frantically searched for them.

In *Dog Days at the White House*, Bryant described the star-crossed lives of the rodents: "There was a family of hamsters, like something out of a Greek tragedy. First, one hamster drowned itself in the president's tub. Then the others were eaten by their father. But the final act beat all—the mother hamster killed the father and then died herself, probably of indigestion."

Then there were the birds. Caroline's yellow canary, named Robin, who liked to perch on President Kennedy's head, also met her demise in the White House—and had a queen pay a visit to her grave. In 1962, when Queen Farah of Iran was visiting the White House, Caroline, then age four, asked her mother to bring the queen to Robin's burial site in the backyard, according to the *Miami News* (as reprinted in Margaret Truman's book *White House Pets*). "That was the one thing Caroline wanted the empress to see," Mrs. Kennedy recounted. The story went on to describe how "the empress, fighting back a smile, expressed suitable sorrow at the grave, near Caroline's play area."

The parakeets, Bluebelle and Maybelle, given to the Kennedys by Lem Billings, lived in a cage in the White House nursery and were John Jr.'s pets, according to the John F. Kennedy Presidential Library and Museum. Mrs. Kennedy, John Jr., and Caroline enjoyed playing with the birds, and a White House photo shows Mrs. Kennedy and Caroline gently cradling one of them, while John Jr. looks on in amazement. When the family had to move out of the White House after the death of President Kennedy, the parakeets went with them.

Two more dogs, with Irish origins, would join the menagerie before the Kennedy presidency ended.

Mrs. Kennedy and Caroline gently cradle one of the White House parakeets, while John Jr. looks on. CECIL W. STOUGHTON, WHITE HOUSE PHOTOGRAPHS. JOHN F. KENNEDY PRESIDENTIAL LIBRARY AND MUSEUM.

At the Fort Myer stables in Arlington, Virginia, in 1963, Caroline feeds the deer that were given to the Kennedys by Irish president Eamon de Valera. John Jr. is on Caroline's right. CECIL W. STOUGHTON, WHITE HOUSE PHOTOGRAPHS. JOHN F. KENNEDY PRESIDENTIAL LIBRARY AND MUSEUM.

## Chapter Six

# A Cherished Gift from Ireland

In 1963 President Kennedy became the first serving president of the United States to visit Ireland, his ancestral homeland. Enormous crowds lined the streets, waving American and Irish flags, step dancing, and singing songs such as "The Boys of Wexford," a ballad about a 1798 Irish rebellion in County Wexford, the home of the president's ancestors. The president was visibly moved by the rapturous welcome.

"From the moment he stepped off the plane, it was love at first sight," recalled special presidential adviser Dave Powers, in his book, *Johnny, We Hardly Knew Ye.* "He fell in love with Ireland and the Irish people fell in love with him. . . . He was one of theirs. He knew it, and they knew it." As he was leaving from Dublin airport, President Kennedy promised to return and bring Mrs. Kennedy (tragically, he would never fulfill this promise). He also quoted a nineteenth-century Irish poem by Gerald Griffin about an emigrant's pain:

*'Tis the Shannon's brightly glancing stream,*
*Brightly gleaming, silent in the morning beam*
*Oh! The sight entrancing*
*Thus return from travels long, years of exile*
*Years of pain*
*To see the Shannon's face again*
*O'er the waters glancing.*

During this trip to Ireland, the president was given two spotted deer by Irish president Eamon de Valera, which stayed at the Fort Myers stables in Arlington, Virginia. (After Kennedy's death, they were given to the National Zoo in Washington, DC.) In Ireland, the president also received the gift of a little English Cocker Spaniel puppy, which he would call Shannon, perhaps inspired by the poem he quoted at Dublin airport.

In an interview with the Kennedy Library, Frances Condell, the mayor of Limerick, described how she presented the president with the puppy. Condell was so enchanted by Ireland's most famous son that she followed him around the

President Kennedy feeds bread to a deer at Lassen Volcanic National Park in California in 1963. The Irish government gave the president two deer of his own as a gift. CECIL W. STOUGHTON, WHITE HOUSE PHOTOGRAPHS. JOHN F. KENNEDY PRESIDENTIAL LIBRARY AND MUSEUM.

country "like a groupie with a rock star." After President Kennedy's speech in Limerick, she gave him the traditional key to the city, followed by the presentation of gifts. "And one he liked particularly was the presentation of the little puppy, Shannon, as a gift for Caroline," Condell recalled.

According to Dave Powers, "President Kennedy turned down all gifts of dogs other than Shannon and Wolf." (Wolf would come later.) Although the president was clearly delighted by the puppy, he was not allowed to take him out of Ireland when he departed on Air Force One because of import restrictions. Shannon would make the trip to the US later.

For years the origin of who provided Shannon to Mayor Condell has been a mystery. It's been speculated that he was a gift from Irish Prime Minister Seán Lemass, Irish President Eamon de Valera, or the descendants of John Barry from Wexford, Ireland. The Jacqueline B. Kennedy files at the John F. Kennedy Library have recently revealed that the puppy was a gift from the famous Parnassus Cocker Spaniel kennels, located in Limerick and owned by Mrs. J. G. Barry.

Her husband was John Barry, a veterinarian and descendant of the famous naval captain John Barry. Widely credited as the "Father of the American Navy" (a moniker he shares with John Paul Jones), Barry was appointed captain in the Continental Navy on December 7, 1775. Following the Revolutionary War, he became America's first commissioned naval officer, at the rank of commodore, receiving his commission from President George Washington in 1797. Commodore Barry was a native of the Kennedy ancestral home of County Wexford, and the president placed a wreath at the John Barry statue during his visit there.

Many books have described Shannon as a Cocker Spaniel or an Irish Spaniel, but the proper identification is that of the familiar English Cocker Spaniel. According to the AKC's *The Complete Dog Book*, the English Cocker Spaniel is "one of the oldest types of land spaniels known, and descended from the original spaniels of Spain as one of a family destined to become highly diversified in size, type, coloring, and hunting ability."

Shannon was descended from championship lines and was sired by Ch. Colinwood Blue Rocket, who was Ireland's 1961 Dog of the Year. Coincidentally, Shannon was born on May 23, 1963—the same day as the Charlie-Pushinka puppies.

On August 8, 1963, Dr. Barry signed the health certificate for Shannon's move to the United States, stating that he was in excellent health and free from all contagious diseases. Shannon arrived at the White House on August 10.

White House social secretary Nancy Tuckerman sent the following letter to the Barry family:

*To the Children of the Barry Family,*
*How very kind of you to send Caroline the little black*
*and white Cocker Spaniel, and we send you our appre-*
*ciation of your thoughtfulness. The puppy arrived at*
*the White House two days ago, and when the President*
*returned to Hyannis Port, he reported the puppy was*
*in good health and withstood the plane flight very well.*
*Needless to say, Caroline can hardly wait to return to*
*Washington to see and play with the puppy, and I am*
*told he is very good natured and sweet looking.*
    *Caroline appreciates this kind gesture so very much*
*and has asked me to send you her thanks.*
    *Sincerely,*
    *Nancy Tuckerman*

With the tragic loss of Patrick Bouvier Kennedy on August 9, the timing of Shannon's arrival could not have been better. According to Sarah Bradford in her book *America's Queen: The Life of Jacqueline Kennedy Onassis*, when the puppy arrived in Washington, President Kennedy looked at him and said, "He looks so sad, I know how he must feel." He then brought the pup to Hyannis Port and presented him to the First Lady, hoping to comfort her.

When Mrs. Kennedy came out of the hospital, Shannon was introduced to Charlie, Clipper, and "the pupniks" at

Shannon when he arrived from Ireland, at Cape Cod in 1963. ROBERT L. KNUDSEN, WHITE HOUSE PHOTOGRAPHS. JOHN F. KENNEDY PRESIDENTIAL LIBRARY AND MUSEUM.

Hyannis Port. Pushinka remained at the White House due to her nervousness.

Shannon quickly endeared himself to the First Family and was given free rein of the White House. Not only was he a link to President Kennedy's unforgettable Ireland trip, but the puppy had a feisty, scrappy personality, challenging all the mastiffs and boxers in Hyannis Port. Even when driven into the ocean, he would bark defiantly from the waves, and the president would cheer him on.

When Mrs. Kennedy, Caroline, and John Jr. left the White House for the final time on December 6, 1963, the only dog

John Jr. plays with Shannon, the English Cocker Spaniel, on Cape Cod in 1963. Shannon was the only dog the Kennedys kept after President Kennedy was assassinated, and became John Jr.'s beloved pet. CECIL W. STOUGHTON, WHITE HOUSE PHOTOGRAPHS. JOHN F. KENNEDY PRESIDENTIAL LIBRARY AND MUSEUM.

that accompanied them was Shannon. Perhaps it was because he was one of the last gifts that President Kennedy had given to Mrs. Kennedy.

Although originally intended as a gift for Caroline, Shannon turned out to be a constant companion to John Jr. In fact, they were so inseparable that Mrs. Kennedy was never sure whom to punish when food went missing or when there was an inexplicable mess in the house.

Hamilton Rowan Jr., an American Kennel Club senior executive at the time, recalled the following encounter with some famous visitors in search of "papers" verifying Shannon's pedigree in a November 21, 2013, retrospective on the AKC website:

> One late afternoon in May, 1970, the elevator door at the AKC's 51 Madison Avenue office clanged open and out walked an impeccably attired lady, followed by an obviously subdued 10-year-old boy. Jacqueline Kennedy Onassis and her son, John F. Kennedy Jr., had arrived at my invitation. One month prior, I had received a telephone call from Mrs. Onassis's secretary, Nancy Tuckerman, asking whether it would be possible to obtain "papers" for John's English Cocker Spaniel. . . .
>
> Mrs. Onassis was anxious to have the now 7-year-old dog sire a litter. Mrs. Onassis, however, was

*adamant that the resultant puppies be eligible for AKC registration.*

*Before being appointed AKC secretary, I had spent a year reorganizing the Foreign Registration department. The knowledge acquired there would now serve me well. I telephoned Dublin and explained the situation to the Irish Kennel Club's registrar, an individual with whom I had established an fine working relationship. One week later, I opened a large envelope from Dublin and spread out on my desk the Irish Kennel Club export pedigree for an English Cocker Spaniel dog, Shannon Kennedy, together with an IKC multi-generation pedigree. As usual, my belief in leprechauns had been justified.*

*After some routine formalities, I had Shannon's registration certificate in hand. I phoned Tuckerman with the good news and meekly added that perhaps Mrs. Onassis might like to have this certificate presented to John at the AKC offices, and at the same time show him our beautiful dog art collection and explain how and why dogs get registered. Not 10 minutes later, Tuckerman called with Mrs. Onassis's enthusiastic acceptance.*

*Knowing Mrs. Onassis's disdain for publicity, and because John was still under Secret Service protection, I suggested she arrive at 5:30 p.m., when only the few AKC night-shift people would be working. I alerted building security about our distinguished guests. Thus, it was by pre-arrangement that security met them at the Madison Avenue entrance and escorted them to an empty, waiting elevator. Virtually no one else was aware of our visitors.*

*During a short meeting in my office, Senior Vice President John Bronwell and I presented John with Shannon's registration certificate, an AKC three-generation certified pedigree, and a copy of* The Complete Dog Book. *Then followed a tour of the executive offices on the 20th floor, including the Library, where both of our guests signed the leather-bound visitors book. Mrs. Onassis was genuinely impressed with our collection of dog art; I think John would have preferred to be home playing with Shannon.*

*When the visit was over, I accompanied Mrs. Onassis and John on the elevator down to the lobby where, to my amazement, a crowd of several hundred people had gathered in the intervening hour. We walked through a gauntlet of applauding onlookers to the sidewalk. On cue, two limousines rolled into view. Two Secret Service agents held the car door open while Mrs. Onassis and John expressed their appreciation to me. And then they were gone.*

The next step was for them to find a female English Cocker Spaniel to breed with Shannon. Mrs. Onassis called upon her good friend and veterinarian, Dr. Lewis Berman, for his advice. Together, they decided to contact Mr. and Mrs. Seymour F. Prager, owner of the notable On Time Farm kennels. Mrs. Prager offered to lease her champion bitch, Ch. On Time Cassandra's Bonnie, to the Kennedys for a fee of $500. The lease agreement would be valid from August 29, 1970, through December 9, 1970. The contract further stipulated that if Bonnie was returned in good health after the litter was weaned, there would be a refund of $250.

On October 29, 1970, a litter of four puppies was born, with two males and two females. Honoring their contract, the kennel owners registered the litter with the American Kennel Club, and John Jr. kept one male blue roan puppy, which he named Whiskey. The young boy was thrilled to have bred his first (and only) litter of puppies, and he maintained a lifelong love of dogs, often preferring their company to that of most people.

## Chapter Seven

# Bright Voice of the Mountains

Shortly after President Kennedy's trip to Ireland, another puppy with deep Irish roots joined the canine pack at the White House. He was an Irish Wolfhound, aptly named Wolf by Caroline because of his imposing size. Wolf is probably the least well-known of the Kennedy family dogs because his time at the White House was so short-lived.

Wolf's saga with the Kennedys began when Father Thomas Kennedy, an Irish priest and breeder of Irish Wolfhounds, sought to give John Jr. one of his puppies. The cleric wrote a letter inquiring about this to the US Ambassador to Ireland, Matthew McCloskey. Father Kennedy, who believed that he was a distant relative of the president, sent the letter on July 15, 1963.

John Jr., Evelyn Lincoln, and President Kennedy with Wolf and Shannon in the Oval Office in 1963. CECIL W. STOUGHTON, WHITE HOUSE PHOTOGRAPHS. JOHN F. KENNEDY PRESIDENTIAL LIBRARY AND MUSEUM.

Ambassador McCloskey contacted Evelyn Lincoln to see whether the First Family would accept the pup. The answer he received was affirmative.

On August 10, 1963, at the request of Patrick Kelly of the American Embassy in Dublin, Dr. Eileen Parkhill, MRCVS, examined the three-month-old Irish Wolfhound pup. In her opinion, he was in good health and free from infectious disease. Two days later, Wolf flew by Aer Lingus to join the president's family—both human and canine.

Irish Wolfhounds are the tallest of all the dog breeds recognized by the American Kennel Club, and a mature wolfhound can weigh between 150 and 160 pounds. Despite its size, the wolfhound is also known for its grace and speed. Because of these attributes, the wolfhound was used as a war dog, trained to pull men off chariots and horses, and also as a guard dog. The wolfhound's size and prowess made it a legendary figure in Irish mythology. Known by the Irish name Cú Faoil, the wolfhound hunted wolves, deer, wild boar, and enormous elk. An old Irish proverb described the breed as "gentle when stroked, fierce when provoked."

Although the Irish Wolfhound is known for its strength, its average life expectancy is only about six to eight years.

Ownership of a prized wolfhound was granted only to Irish nobility, including poets and storytellers. They were also presented as gifts to kings and princes throughout the world.

——— FORM No. 2 ———

Cumann na Ṡaórⱥiṫeⱥċⱥ Ṡⱥeḃeⱥlⱥiṡe
(THE IRISH KENNEL CLUB)

# REGISTRATION CERTIFICATE

## This is to Certify

No. 106,625

That on ......13th November, 1963...................................... a ...n Irish Wolfhound
....(Greywhite toes).........

has been registered by the name of

"GLOR    GEAL    NA SLEIBTE" (Litter)

the Owner ......Rev. Thomas Kennedy........................................................ having

supplied the particulars of pedigree, which have been entered in the Registers.

Sex ...Male............... Date of Birth..................19th May, 1963
"JAN OF BALLYGRAN"(91,803)

Sire ..................................................................................

"LITTLE MO OF BALLYGRAN"(87,024)

Dam ..................................................................................

Owner.

Breeder..........................................................................................

*This Certificate is an acknowledgment of the payment of the registration fee.*

*If the above particulars are not correct in every detail, this*    MAUD C. FOX, per..................
*Certificate should be returned immediately for amendment.*    Secretary.

(vertical text in right margin: DATE ISSUED )

Wolf's registration certificate from the Irish Kennel Club in 1963, with his Irish
name, Glor Geal Na Sleibte, which means "Bright Voice of the Mountains."
JACQUELINE BOUVIER KENNEDY ONASSIS PERSONAL PAPERS. JOHN F. KENNEDY
PRESIDENTIAL LIBRARY AND MUSEUM.

Facing page: John Jr. and Evelyn Lincoln, President Kennedy's secretary, feed biscuits
to Shannon and Wolf, with Clipper in the foreground, on the White House grounds
in 1963. CECIL W. STOUGHTON, WHITE HOUSE PHOTOGRAPHS. JOHN F. KENNEDY
PRESIDENTIAL LIBRARY AND MUSEUM.

Oliver Cromwell eventually put an end to this in 1652 by enacting a law banning the wolfhound's export because the breed was dwindling.

The wolfhound grew so deeply enshrined in Ireland's culture that it became a symbol for the country itself, appearing on everything from the coats of arms of early Irish kings to Belleek china and the Irish sixpence. A mournful statue of a wolfhound commemorates the deaths of the Civil War soldiers of the Irish Brigade at Gettysburg National Battlefield in Gettysburg, Pennsylvania.

The Kennedys' wolfhound was a male brindle pup, born on May 19, 1963, at the home of Father Kennedy at St. Brigid's in Rosenallis, County Laois, Ireland. Wolf was registered by the Irish Kennel Club with the name Glor Geal Na Sleibte, which in Irish means "Bright Voice of the Mountains."

Wolf was placed aboard Aer Lingus Flight 107 on August 12, 1963, destined for New York's Idlewild airport (which would later be renamed John F. Kennedy International Airport following his death in 1963). Upon his arrival at Idlewild, the young wolfhound was put on yet another plane that would arrive at the Barnstable County Airport in Massachusetts. His destination was Brambletyde, the summer White House on Squaw Island. Here the pup was met by White House kennel master Bryant. All shipping arrangements were made through Ambassador Matthew McCloskey.

**AER LINGUS**

## Le Dea-Mhéin
## with compliments

*8/12/63*

*Dear Sir,*
*Please find attached*
*the documents you require. Also*
*please note the [...] cert.*

*[...] will follow by post.*

*yours truly,*
*D. T. Kelly*

0896-35M-9/62-B.

Correspondence about Wolf in 1963. JACQUELINE BOUVIER KENNEDY ONASSIS
PERSONAL PAPERS. JOHN F. KENNEDY PRESIDENTIAL LIBRARY AND MUSEUM

The children's nanny, Maud Shaw, recalled that Caroline took one look at the strapping gray-and-black puppy and promptly named him "Wolfie." He quickly integrated himself into the Kennedy canine pack and prowled confidently around the wide lawn next to the Atlantic Ocean, no doubt oblivious to the fact that he had recently come across the "pond" to a grand new life. One of his first trips was to Ambassador Kennedy's stables in Osterville, Massachusetts,

**R. H. LAMBERT & SON**

PARTNERS

N. H. LAMBERT, m.r.c.v.s.

EILEEN PARKHILL, m.r.c.v.s.

*47 South Richmond Street, Dublin.*

SURGERY Hours : 9.30 a.m. to 1 p.m.

2.30 p.m. to 5.30 p.m. (Except Saturday)

PHONE 51222.

I hereby certify that at the request of Mr. Patrick Kelly, American Embassy Dublin. I have this day examined a male brindle Irish Wolfhound aged about two months.

In my opinion this dog is in good health and free from infectious and contagious diseases.

Signed........................

Letter from Dr. Eileen Parkhill, a Dublin vet, certifying that Wolf was in good health in 1963. JACQUELINE BOUVIER KENNEDY ONASSIS PERSONAL PAPERS. JOHN F. KENNEDY PRESIDENTIAL LIBRARY AND MUSEUM.

Facing page: Letter to Matthew McCloskey, Ambassador to Ireland, from Mary Gallagher, Mrs. Kennedy's secretary, in 1963 asking for Wolf's papers, which were lost when he flew to the US. In the letter, Mrs. Gallagher describes Wolf as a "wonderful dog." JACQUELINE BOUVIER KENNEDY ONASSIS PERSONAL PAPERS. JOHN F. KENNEDY PRESIDENTIAL LIBRARY AND MUSEUM.

The Honorable Matthew McCloskey
c/o McCloskey & Son
1620 Thompson Street
Philadelphia, Pennsylvania

Dear Ambassador:

Last year, an Irish Wolfhound was sent to
President Kennedy through you -- I believe
it came from a Father Kennedy in Dublin.
Unfortunately, his papers were lost en route.
As he is a wonderful dog, and a very good one,
it is so important to get his papers so that
I can register him here.

I wondered if it would be possible for you
either to send me a copy of his original
papers -- or, if that is too complicated,
and you will be leaving for the summer,
could you tell me how to get in touch with
his breeder so that I could get the papers
that way.

It would help greatly if your reply to me
could be marked - "Attention: Mary Gallagher".

I do thank you so much.  My best wishes to you
and to Mrs. McCloskey.

                    Sincerely,

June 16, 1964

where he liked to follow the family ponies, Macaroni, Leprechaun, and Tex, as if they were his littermates. In fact, many people at the stables thought he was a small pony when they first saw him.

Wolf would remain at the Cape until the family returned to the White House following the Labor Day weekend. It quickly became apparent to all that although Wolf was affable with people, he had an aversion to other dogs—especially Clipper.

President Kennedy grew quite fond of Wolf, and this was evident when the dog received unprecedented access to the Oval Office during Halloween 1963. Caroline and John Jr. had come for a visit to show their costumes to their father. The beaming president and the children posed for a photo, and then the president called for the dogs to be brought to his office—but only Wolf appeared. Evidently Wolf could not resist, because he so thoroughly enjoyed the dog biscuits that the president kept in his HMS *Resolute* desk.

When his schedule permitted, the president would often step outside his office and offer biscuits to Wolf and the other dogs in an area near the Rose Garden. In her book, *My Twelve Years with John F. Kennedy*, Evelyn Lincoln included an anecdote about the president and his attempts to feed his dogs:

Caroline with Wolf and Macaroni at Atoka in 1963. CECIL W. STOUGHTON, WHITE HOUSE PHOTOGRAPHS. JOHN F. KENNEDY PRESIDENTIAL LIBRARY AND MUSEUM.

*Now that we had four dogs [including Wolf] chasing each other around the South Lawn, the President decided to get some dog food and feed them himself. For the next few days, whenever he had a free moment and*

Caroline and President Kennedy with the ponies Macaroni and Tex at the walkway from the West Wing to the South Lawn of the White House in 1963. ROBERT L. KNUDSEN, WHITE HOUSE PHOTOGRAPHS. JOHN F. KENNEDY PRESIDENTIAL LIBRARY AND MUSEUM.

Facing page: Mrs. Kennedy and John Jr. hold the puppies from Pushinka and Charlie's litter while Caroline bonds with Wolf on Cape Cod in 1963. CECIL W. STOUGHTON, WHITE HOUSE PHOTOGRAPHS. JOHN F. KENNEDY PRESIDENTIAL LIBRARY AND MUSEUM.

*the dogs were near his office, he went on the portico
and clapped his hands. But the dogs didn't know that
he was the president, and they paid no attention to
him. John-John came out and asked if he could feed
them. The president said, "No, I am going to feed them,
when they are over here." But the dogs were used to
John and they went to him instead of the President.*

*After several more tries, President Kennedy finally
got three of the dogs into the office, and they began to
eat out of his hand. A little later, he walked through
my office on his way to the mansion, the dogs right at
his heels. He looked as pleased as a little boy that he had
won them over. "And I didn't need to put them on a leash
to have them follow me," he said. It was a well-known
fact that President Kennedy truly loved dogs, more so
than First Lady Jacqueline Kennedy whose passion was
for horses.*

With his natural curiosity and penchant for learning
about all things that existed in his world, President Kennedy
sought information about Wolf's bloodline that went deep
into Ireland's past. On November 3, 1963, following mass

Facing page: John Jr. holds a turtle as he walks toward a snoozing Wolf and Clipper at the family retreat in Atoka, Virginia, in 1964. The two large dogs did not always get along well. CECIL W. STOUGHTON, WHITE HOUSE PHOTOGRAPHS. JOHN F. KENNEDY PRESIDENTIAL LIBRARY AND MUSEUM.

Caroline and Mrs. Kennedy visit with her horse, Sardar, at the Fort Meyer stables in Arlington, Virginia, in 1962. Sardar was given to Mrs. Kennedy by Pakistani President Mohammed Ayub Khan.
CECIL W. STOUGHTON, WHITE HOUSE PHOTOGRAPHS.
JOHN F. KENNEDY PRESIDENTIAL LIBRARY AND MUSEUM.

at St. Stephen's Church near his home in Atoka, Virginia, President Kennedy and his family paid a visit to Henry B. Weaver's 110 Glengyle Farm in Aldie, Virginia. Weaver was a renowned exhibitor of champion Irish Wolfhounds and a prominent corporate lawyer, serving as the general counsel for the Atlantic-Richfield Oil Company, which would later become ARCO. Presumably, the president left with a keener understanding of his own Irish Wolfhound and his storied ancestry.

When Mrs. Kennedy and the children left the White House for the final time on December 6, 1963, most of the dogs had been placed with family friends. Wolf stayed at the Kennedys' home in Atoka until May of 1964, and then the "gentle giant" found a new home with a family in Middleburg, Virginia. It was fitting that the last dog of the Kennedy presidency was a regal emblem of Ireland.

—

Anatole France wrote, "Until one has loved an animal, a part of one's soul remains unawakened." The love of animals marked the lives of the Kennedy family, and their history was closely entwined with that of their various pets.

# AFTERWORD

## By Margaret Reed, PhD

President Harry S. Truman famously said, "If you want a friend in Washington, get a dog." President John F. Kennedy did just that. The story goes that God said to him, "I have good news and bad. The good news is that you will be permitted to bring your dog, your cat, or whatever to the White House—there is no lease restriction." "Oh thank you, Sir," said the new president, "and what is the bad news?" "The bad news is that the dog will be happier than you." When Kennedy arrived at the White House in January 1961, he had one dog, and at the time of his untimely passing on November 22, 1963, he had acquired a pack of nine dogs.

Senator Ted Kennedy told me on the evening of the JFK Library's annual dinner in May 2008 that he and his brothers "were crazy about dogs because they have a hopeful spirit; they're smart, resilient, determined, and optimistic." Like his father before him, John Kennedy was proud of his Irish heritage but refused to be defined by it. He was well aware of the prejudice and discrimination he would face as an Irish

American Catholic who sought to be the thirty-fifth president of the United States. Even so, he was outgoing, affable, charming, stylish, and handsome and had all the gifts with the exception of time. He touched the lives of many, including mine, through his kindness and genuine love of dogs.

The research for this book started in January of 2010. I had no idea the twists and turns that life would take in the ensuing years and the persistent realization that the book might never be completed. My primary goal was not about publishing another Kennedy book but more of a personal quest: to find out exactly what had happened to President Kennedy's dogs following that sad day in November of 1963.

When I read Robert Dallek's *An Unfinished Life*, an excellent book on the life of our thirty-fifth president, I thought about my own project, which was an unfinished book. So much had happened in my personal life but most importantly was the loss of my mother, who had encouraged me to write the story. After the grief had passed and the settling of her estate had been completed, her words came roaring back loud and clear: "Don't start something you're not prepared to finish!" Realizing that I needed assistance to finish what I had started, I contacted my good friend, Joan Lownds, who was a successful journalist and author, and asked her to join me on this journey. She was generous enough to agree, and we started the work immediately.

There's a photograph of President Kennedy standing outside the Oval Office with his back turned away from the camera and a German Shepherd standing in front of him. The dog is Clipper, at the time the family's most recent acquisition to the Kennedy Canine Corps. The photograph certainly isn't of award-winning quality, but what makes it so appealing is what it portrays: the leader of the Free World holding a box of dog biscuits and obviously having a brief but nevertheless personal encounter with one of his pets. The photo humanizes a powerful man and provides us with an image that all of us can relate to, proving that dogs truly are the greatest of all equalizers. Lord Byron, in his devotional phrase to his beloved Newfoundland, wrote, "Strength without Insolence, Courage without Ferocity, And all the Virtues of man without his Vices." Dogs have consistently displayed the finest qualities of humans and few, if any, of the negative ones. President Kennedy recognized this from an early age and embraced it his entire life.

There is no doubt that President Kennedy observed that the friendship of a dog oftentimes put his friendship with associates to shame. In the company of his dogs, he could actually be himself and not worry if what he said would be reported in the press the following day. Science proves that dogs have an intense affinity for humans, understanding when we are sad and rejoicing when we are happy. Studies show that the mere presence of a dog can reduce stress and lower blood pressure. Perhaps President Kennedy knew this when he called for his Welsh Terrier, Charlie, to be brought to the White House while contemplating the Cuban missile crisis.

In October 2016, following the annual Robert F. Kennedy Golf Tournament, Chris and Sheila Kennedy were kind enough to invite us to Brambletyde, President Kennedy's onetime summer White House in Hyannis Port. Brambletyde is an amazing, quintessential Cape Cod home, rich with history, which sits high upon a bluff and overlooks the expansive Nantucket Sound. The last time I had been there was in 1963 when President Kennedy was vacationing with his family and all his dogs.

It was a magnificent evening, complete with a glorious harvest moon. As I stood on that bluff overlooking Lewis Bay, I closed my eyes and could clearly see the dogs of Camelot dashing around on that lush, green lawn and the people who made a difference in my life. The bark of a dog in the distance snapped me back to reality and set me back on the path of finishing what had started years ago. In that moment, I discovered that sometimes we need to revisit our past memories before we can actually move forward.

# ACKNOWLEDGMENTS

John F. Kennedy inspired and touched the lives of many people during his brief time as our thirty-fifth president. Many of these individuals have been instrumental in the compilation of this book. I am forever grateful to them for their assistance, generosity, and patience and for providing the facts that might otherwise have been lost to history. Ambassador Caroline Kennedy has often said that her father's time is becoming part of history rather than living memory. I'm thankful that President Kennedy touched my life and provided a memory that has lasted a lifetime.

The John F. Kennedy Presidential Library and Museum is an inspiring memorial to President Kennedy and is staffed by an amazing group of knowledgeable individuals who have complete command of the president's records, documents, files, photographs, and films that preserve the memories of the Kennedy administration. I am deeply indebted to the archivists and staff, most notably audiovisual archivist Laurie Austin, whose research and knowledge of the Kennedy photo collection contributed so much to this book. To archivists Stephen Plotkin, Alan Goodrich, and Abigail Malangone, your patience in answering all our questions and locating records has proved invaluable.

Sincerest thanks to Tom McNaught, former executive director of the John F. Kennedy Library Foundation, for his encouragement and for seeing the potential for such a book. Special thanks to US Secret Service agent Clint Hill (retired) and Lisa McCubbin for their advice, assistance, and work on the foreword of the book. Your expertise made all the difference.

To those who were witnesses to history, Senator Ted Kennedy, Ann Gargan King, Ted Sorenson, Richard Donahue, John Siegenthaler, Burke Marshall, Tish Baldrige, Peggy Foster, Secret Service agent Tom Wells, Katherine Paramore, Doug Fout, Dr. Arthur Bernstein, DVM, Dr. Lewis Berman, DVM, and especially Nancy Tuckerman, I offer my undying gratitude for sharing your lifetime of experience and memories.

Most books have research assistants who are the unsung heroes of any project, and I am grateful to the voices of reason Karen Ang, Jory Lockwood, and Logan Varsano, who were integral to the fact-finding for *The Dogs of Camelot*. American Kennel Club president Dennis Sprung provided the full resources of the AKC registry and library for additional research.

# Acknowledgments

The driving force of my coauthor, Joan Lownds, and Lyons Press senior editor Holly Rubino kept the project on track and focused. You will always hold a special place in my heart for believing in this project and seeing it through to its completion. To our wonderful agent, Adam Chromy of Movable Type Management, we thank you for your hard work, dedication, and expertise.

My soul companion, Patti Fernandes, who has been there every step of the way during this incredible journey—thank you for encouraging me to follow my passion. Finally, to my mom, Patricia Walsh Reed, who provided the opportunity to experience history firsthand and for your love, strength, and belief that I really could finish what I started.

# SOURCES

*Alexandria Gazette.* Tom Kitten's obituary. August 21, 1962.

American Kennel Club. "The Welsh Terrier." October 29, 2014. www.akc.org/dog-breeds/welsh-terrier.

———. *The Complete Dog Book.* New York: Ballantine Books, 2006.

*American Kennel Club Gazette.* "Shannon Gets His Papers: The Day the Kennedys Came to the AKC." November 1999.

———. Breed Columns, "Welsh Terrier." 1961 Archives.

Andersen, Christopher. *Sweet Caroline: Last Child of Camelot.* New York: Harper Collins, 2003.

Bradford, Sarah. *America's Queen: The Life of Jacqueline Kennedy Onassis.* New York: Penguin Group, 2000.

Bradlee, Ben. *Conversations with Kennedy.* New York: W. W. Norton and Company, 1975.

Bryant, Traphes, and Spatz Frances Leighton. *Dog Days at the White House: The Outrageous Memoirs of the Presidential Kennel Keeper.* New York: Macmillan, 1998.

*Chicago Tribune.* "Caroline Runs Hamster Hunt in White House: Staff Helps Search for Her Two Lost Pets." March 1961.

Clifton, V. Chester, Cecil Stoughton, and Hugh Sidey. *The Memories: JFK 1961–1963*. New York: W. W. Norton and Company, 1980.

Dallek, Robert. *An Unfinished Life: John F. Kennedy, 1917–1963*. New York: Time Warner Book Group, 2003.

Driscoll, Laura. *Presidential Pets*. New York: Penguin Group, 2009.

Espy, Hilda Cole. "Dogs, Cats, Birds, Fish, Small, Furry Animals, Creepers, Leapers and Crawlers and Many Others: A Charming Story about Caroline Kennedy and Her Pets." *Woman's Day*, July 1962.

Fay, Paul B. Jr. *The Pleasure of His Company*. New York: Harper & Row, 1966.

Fitzgerald, Thomas A. Jr. *Grandpa Stories*. Aurora, CO: Rundel Park Press, 2006.

Galbraith, John Kenneth. *Ambassador's Journal: A Personal Account of the Kennedy Years*. Boston: Houghton Mifflin, 1966.

Goodwin, Doris Kearns. *The Fitzgeralds and the Kennedys: An American Saga*. New York: Simon and Schuster, 1987.

Haggerty, Bridget. "The Irish Wolfhound—A Brief History." Irish Cultures and Customs. Accessed August 30, 2016. www.irishcultureandcustoms.com/AEmblem/Wolfhound.html.

Hamilton, Nigel. *JFK: Reckless Youth*. New York: Random House, 1992.

Hill, Clinton, and Lisa McCubbin. *Me and Mrs. Kennedy*. New York: Simon and Schuster, 2012.

Irish Wolfhound Club of America. Accessed September 24, 2016. www.iwclubofamerica.org/index.html.

Kennedy, Caroline. Interview by Jon Stewart. *The Daily Show with Jon Stewart*, Comedy Central, September 15, 2011.

Kennedy, Edward M. *True Compass*. New York: Hachette Books, 2009.

Kennedy, Jacqueline. Interview by Arlene Francis. *Home*, NBC, April 3, 1957. www.youtube.com/watch?v=XebG54eybsc.

Kennedy, John F. Jr. Interview by Larry King. *Larry King Live*, CNN, September 28, 1995.

Lincoln, Evelyn. *My Twelve Years with John F. Kennedy*. New York: David McKay Company, 1965.

Manchester, William. *The Death of a President*. New York: Harper & Row, 1967.

O'Donnell, Kenneth P., and David F. Powers, with Joe McCarthy. *Johnny, We Hardly Knew Ye: Memories of John Fitzgerald Kennedy*. Boston: Little, Brown, 1970.

Pitts, David. *Jack and Lem: John F. Kennedy and Lem Billings; The Untold Story of an Extraordinary Friendship.* New York: Carroll and Graf Publishers, 2007.

Presidential Pet Museum. "Robin: Caroline Kennedy's Pet Canary." January 6, 2004. www.presidentialpetmuseum .com/pets/caroline-kennedy-canary.

Reeves, Richard. *President Kennedy: Profile of Power.* New York: Simon & Schuster, 1993.

Rowan, Roy, and Brooke Janis. *First Dogs: American Presidents and Their Best Friends.* Chapel Hill, NC: Algonquin Books, 1997.

Salinger, Pierre. *With Kennedy.* Garden City, NY: Doubleday, 1966.

Schlesinger, Arthur M., Jr. *A Thousand Days.* Boston: Houghton Mifflin, 1965.

Shaw, Mark. *The John F. Kennedys: A Family Album.* Toronto: Ambassador Books, 1964.

Shaw, Maud. *White House Nannie: My Years with Caroline and John Kennedy, Jr.* New York: New American Library, 1965.

Smith, Merriman. Story for United Press International, January 1963.

Sorenson, Theodore C. *Kennedy.* New York: Harper and Row, 1965.

Thayer, Mary Van Rensselaer. *Jacqueline Bouvier Kennedy.* Garden City, NY: Doubleday, 1961.

Truman, Margaret. *White House Pets.* New York: David McKay Company, 1969.

Tubridy, Ryan. *JFK in Ireland: Four Days That Changed a President.* Guilford, CT: Globe Pequot Press, 2013.

Turner, Jim. "John F. Kennedy Was an Arizona Cowboy." Accessed July 28, 2016. http://jimturnerhistorian.org/john_f_kennedy_was_an_arizona_cowboy.

*Washington Post.* "Prestige Is Going to the Dogs in the Nation's Capitol." May 15, 1963.

West, J. B., with Mary Lynn Kotz. *Upstairs at the White House.* New York: Coward, McCann & Geoghegan, 1973.

Widmer, Ted. *Listening In: The Secret White House Recordings of John F. Kennedy.* New York: Hyperion Books, 2012.

*World Heritage Encyclopedia.* Accessed June 15, 2016. http://worldjournals.org/articles/Belka_and_Strelka.

## AUTHOR INTERVIEWS/CONVERSATIONS

Letitia Baldrige, March 2009

Dr. Lewis Berman, February 2012 and July 2014

Dr. Arthur Bernstein, March 2013

Sally Cottingham Fay, August 2016

Margaret Foster, July 2010

Doug Fout, November 2011

Alan Goodrich, Archivist, John F. Kennedy Presidential Library, November 2010 and January 2012

Clint Hill, US Secret Service (retired), April 2017

Edward Kennedy, May 2008

John F. Kennedy Jr., February 1996

Ann Gargan King, February 2011

Katherine Foster Parramore, January 2011 and January 2015

John Seigenthaler, May 2009 and May 2012

Ted Sorenson, May 2010

Nancy Tuckerman, May 2012, August 2012, February 2013, November 2013, and August 2014

Tom Wells, US Secret Service (retired), July 2010

Irvin Williams, November 2016

### JOHN F. KENNEDY PRESIDENTIAL LIBRARY AND MUSEUM ORAL HISTORY PROGRAM

Janet Auchincloss, September 6, 1964

Traphes Bryant, May 13, 1964

David Burke, April 17, 1979

George C. Burkley, October 17, 1967

Barbara J. Coleman, October 24, 1969

Frances P. Condell, July 31, 1967

Paul B. Fay, February 15, 1971

Richard Flood, December 12, 1964

Priscilla Harris letter to Edward M. Kennedy, December 12, 1969

Ann Lincoln, February 9, 1965

Maud Shaw, April 27, 1965

Nancy L. Tuckerman, October 30, 1964

Pamela Turnure, October 30, 1964

William Walton, October 3, 1963

J. Bernard West, Chief White House Usher, 1967

Elmer Young and James Nelson, June 11, 1964

### JOHN F. KENNEDY PRESIDENTIAL LIBRARY AND MUSEUM DOG RECORDS

Digitized Folder of Material

Subject Files: Dog records: Port Fortune Sarah's Ben. Jacqueline Bouvier Kennedy Onassis Personal Papers, May 1960: 5–21. This file contains a dog license, American Kennel Club certificate of registration, and certificate of pedigree regarding Port Fortune's Sarah's Ben, a Welsh Terrier later known as Charlie.

Subject Files: Dog records: Pushinka. Jacqueline Bouvier Kennedy Onassis Personal Papers, June 15, 1961–March 5, 1963. This file contains correspondence and vaccination information regarding the mixed breed dog Pushinka, a gift from Soviet Premier Nikita Khrushchev to President John F. Kennedy and his family.

Subject Files: Dog records: Clipper. Jacqueline Bouvier Kennedy Onassis Personal Papers, August 24, 1962– July 26, 1963. This file includes veterinary notes and records, dog licenses, vaccination certificates, and a certificate of pedigree regarding First Lady Jacqueline Kennedy's dog, Clipper, a German Shepherd.

Subject Files: Dog records: Shannon. Jacqueline Bouvier Kennedy Onassis Personal Papers, May 26, 1963– April 30, 1970. This file contains dog licenses, a certificate of pedigree, and letters regarding the dog Shannon, a Cocker Spaniel, a gift from the Barry family in Caherconlish, County Limerick, Ireland, to Caroline Kennedy.

Subject Files: Dog records: Wolf. Jacqueline Bouvier Kennedy Onassis Personal Papers, August 12, 1963–June 23, 1964. This file contains correspondence and records regarding the dog Wolf, an Irish Wolfhound, a gift from Father Thomas Kennedy of Ireland to President John F. Kennedy and his family.

# INDEX